Searching for the
White Magician

Searching for the White Magician

Spiritual Psychology
and the
Manifestation of Destiny

Stefania Magidson
in Dialogue with
Carmen Firan

All rights reserved. Published by New Meridian, part of the non-profit organization New Meridian Arts, 2017.

LIBRARY OF CONGRESS CATALOGING-IN-PUBLICATION DATA
Searching for the White Magician
Stefania Magidson in Dialogue with Carmen Firan
ISBN: 978-0997603866
LCCN: 2017951792

≈

Acknowledgements

Thank you to those who supported this project, whether with advice, ideas or enthusiasm: Mary Hulnick, Diana Cosma, Iulia Şchiopu, Adrian Sângeorzan, Livia & Ştefan Pruteanu, Ana-Maria Pruteanu, Mark Magidson, Michael & David Magidson, Mia Struteanu, Guita Tahmasebi, Aura Cercel, Subir Trivedi. My gratitude to writer and editor Nava Renek for her interest in the topics of this book.

CONTENTS

Introduction

I met Stefania Magidson in New York, many years ago, during a live auction whose proceeds were going to help impoverished Romanian children. Among those present (businessmen, artists, American and Romanian personalities), my attention was drawn toward a young and delicate woman who exuded equally self-confidence, femininity, force and humility and who was bidding generously on the complete works of Andrei Codrescu (himself present among the guests). Someone who chooses a writer's complete collection over offers to exotic island vacations or meals in upscale restaurants deserves one's acquaintance. From that evening on, we became instant friends—as it often happens when people discover mutual affinities and instinctive attractions beyond the convenience of random encounters and the ordinary rhythms of closeness.

Over the years, I discovered in Stefania Magidson a passionate explorer of spiritual adventure, a person dedicated to the exploration of the self, of one's peers and the world, a promoter of harmony and tolerance. She is the perfect balance of intelligence and kindness, artistic sensibility and pragmatism, yet she is without ostentation.

Since arriving in America, I have met many successful immigrants—some talented, others lucky—but Stefania embodies the symbol of succeeding "beyond the five senses," as perhaps she would say herself. She has reinvented herself in her new world while aiming for the top, and, after reaching a platform where she could afford to uplift others, she did not hesitate to do so. Because of her, I started to wonder if our destiny can be seduced, provoked, contradicted, reformulated, turned upside down and made to work in our favor.

With her delicate and mysterious smile, with her elegant and guileless gestures, Stefania confirmed to me that the secret of success, the choices we make on our destiny's path, an entity of air connected to ether with a thin and spiraled thread, resides in our souls and minds. Together they can change our universe: both inner and outer. And I have not only believed her, but found myself immersed in a passionate conversation which, over time, became an entire book. A book which takes on diverse themes, from the roles of institutions to the meaning of our lives, from the challenges of immigration to the role of philanthropy, from religion and spirituality, to self-exploration, all of which, I believe, can inspire readers to find resources and paths that lead to spiritual growth and success on the trajectory of their own self-realization.

Initially I had my heart set on an interview focusing on Stefania's passion for spiritual psychology and the activities of the foundation she leads. However, her unconventional, elaborate answers opened new doors and incited new questions, pushing our dialogue into uncharted and provocative territory. We met several times in New York and Los Angeles and then in Aspen where, during an autumn suffused with honeyed light, we spent days wandering the neighboring paths and browsing through Stefania's photo albums and journals, all witnesses to a bygone communist era.

Our unassuming conversations became a series of several articles published in *Romanian Writing*, a magazine, and over time, the essays became a book. The book explores diverse themes, from the role of institutions to personal purpose, from religion and spirituality to self-exploration. It is a book that I believe will inspire the reader to discover inner resources and paths to spiritual growth, which in turn can serve as catalysts for self-advancement.

I want to frame this dialogue in Stefania's words under the practicality of a motto extracted from the field of spiritual psychology which she studied and which she has applied into her own existential transformation: "Let us choose a dream we've always had and transform it into reality."

Carmen Firan
New York, 2013

Preface

TO THE READERS:
WHO IS THE WHITE MAGICIAN?

We are spiritual beings having a human experience.

I've encountered the White Magician inside of me from the time I was a little girl, while swinging on the swing in the garden, where the endless hours spent in nature, often alone, would transport me to a world that seemed more real and more powerful than that of our usual senses of touch and hearing, of sight, taste and smell. The prayers, the angels and the saints whom my grandparents talked about, along with the discovery in our attic of the American book *The Power of Autosuggestion*[1] added another facet to the body of life notions taking shape inside of me. Indeed, these paradigms were very different from the ones that surrounded me in communist Romania during the '70s.

The fact that I set foot in America at the trying age of fifteen and the necessity to start from ground zero

---

[1] The book was left there by my Transylvanian great-grandfather, who lived in New York from 1907 to 1957. His many years of American citizenship created a credible basis for our immigration to the US in 1983.

during a political time when leaving Romania was a one-way ticket, forced me to face a blank canvas. My instinct told me I could paint it however I wanted, had I only the strength of self-discovery and the courage to express, in the reality of the five senses, that which I fathomed in my inner world. Over time, from discovering Mircea Eliades's *Forbidden Forest* and Joseph Campbell's *The Power of the Myth* and from reading books and articles by a wide array of Indian swamis, Buddhist teachers, enlightened scientists and shamans, I slowly began to understand a sliver of the nature of the invisible laws that connect us. I was enthralled by the possibility of exploring the mystery and magic of life. Those books were a confirmation that a world beyond our five senses existed; the texts became a bridge between my old life and my new one. The connections and coincidences which I started to observe between my thoughts, aspirations, intuitions, dreams and actual reality made me deeply aware of the connection between the seen and unseen world. I developed a hunger that was temporarily assuaged by the completion of a master's degree in applied spiritual psychology. I consider that much of what I have accomplished in my life, in particular since obtaining my master's degree, is a direct result of conscious inner intentions and conjured dreams.

In 2011, at Carmen's invitation, I started a dialogue for *Romanian Writing* Magazine and over months it took the shape of a possible book. At that time, I was completing a post-masters in "Consciousness, Health and Healing" at University of Santa Monica and hesitated to collaborate, worried I would not be able to cope with the demands of a busy family life, school and running a non-profit foundation. "Come on Stefania," Carmen said, "at least one article per month, and by the end of the fall we can have the entire book." She was right; the courses I was taking offered me not only the perfect backdrop to convey my message, but also gave me the unequaled joy of seeing many of the ideas and concepts presented in our dialogue put into practice right before my very eyes.

The White Magician is that Higher Self inside of us which understands the subtle notions of the universe and is in direct contact with our intuition, that side of us which has access to what is available beyond the five senses. It is the part of us that becomes cognizant, in the beginning instinctively, and then consciously, of our sacred mission in this life. It is the part that has the know-how to explore and the courage to fulfill that which we are meant to accomplish, so that we are reconciled and at peace with the meaning of our existence.

I invite the reader to join me on a journey of exploration and rediscovery of that inner place that holds the lens of mystery and magic through which life filters, if we allow it. I invite him to find that magic wand that transforms inner worlds into realities whose potential is only temporarily dormant.

Stefania Magidson
Los Angeles, 2012

A Grain in a Giant's Pocket

Carmen Firan: *When we become aware of the immense, even infinite, expanse of existence, it is easy to become demoralized and slip towards indifference, passivity, abandonment or cynicism. How can one repress the feeling of uselessness as one comes to terms with the fact that one may be a grain in a giant's pocket?*

Stefania Magidson: The notion that we may be nothing but a small grain in an enormous desert and the ideas of "What do I matter?" or "What influence can I possibly have on the enormity of this desert?" are notions that can be analyzed from many angles, endlessly. It is perhaps nothing less than overwhelming to come to terms with how small and insignificant we may be…This perhaps is what forces me to focus mainly on my "own universe," knowing deeply that the majority of us are nothing but very small waves in a vast ocean, which, however, affect in the subtlest and sometimes unknown ways the bigger waves and the rhythm of the whole.

I believe we are all part of a divine matrix and that we influence each other through every little act we commit, through every word we say and every thought we have, be they conscious or unconscious; these thoughts, words and deeds trigger reactions in the physical and the intangible universe. Having experienced the accuracy of this concept on a daily basis, I have come to understand the significance of the intentions we carry within. This has led me to develop a deep sense of the importance of becoming conscious of my inner intentions, given that they are automatically followed by thoughts and actions which have consequences and produce tangible results. I have also come to learn that, when we have conflicting intentions, the one that has the most energy charge wins.

CF: *Are there exercises for acceptance of our existence, the way it is, with its limits, a way of coming to terms with reality, with lost dreams, with frustrations or failures?*

SM: Perhaps through prayer or meditation. In my experience, when one prays, one petitions God and when one meditates—when we sit quietly and consciously awake in silence—we listen to Divinity's answer, the answer of that universal consciousness, the breath of creation which allows life to be sustained and unfold in every moment. During those moments, my intentions become clear, and I become quite conscious of the possible outcomes of my thoughts, the consequences of my acts.

CF: *In a possible hierarchy of the questions that haunt us on the theme of existence, which do you consider the most important?*

SM: I automatically think that the question at the top is the one that, most probably, haunts most of us, and which I do not consider to be cliché: "What is the meaning of our existence?"

CF: *Are there collateral questions which sustain the intensity of the aforementioned one?*

SM: Absolutely. Who are we beyond our physical body, our thoughts and our feelings? Where in our human body does our soul reside? If energy can be neither created nor destroyed, where does the energy present in our body and consciousness go when it leaves our mortal coil?

CF: *How did you arrive at these questions, or when did you become conscious of them, beyond your academic background?*

SM: Up until the age of six I was raised in turn by my paternal and maternal grandparents, not an uncommon practice among families living under the communist regime[2]. As many kids my age, I spent

---

[2] Like many families after the Soviet occupation, my parents became part of the proletariat and could no longer afford a nanny, but they remained "affluent and thoughtful" enough to look down on state-run nurseries.

most of my time in the countryside, often alone in nature, close to animals, close to the smell of grass and the earth, away from the early analytical, academic methods of modern kindergarten classrooms. In those times, I had a number of transcending experiences that I decoded later, and which made me feel that something palpable connects us with the universe. During the days when I was lying in the grass and watching the clouds go by against the backdrop of a blindingly blue sky, or the night times when I'd abandon myself, soaking in the world of the myriad stars that filled my spectrum of vision, my yearning to close the gap of the infinite distances of the cosmos—to feel at home and authentically a part of it—was piercing.

Another memory that hasn't left me is the morning my grandmother sent me to feed our chickens the crumbs left over from breakfast. As I reached for these crumbs and threw them to the hungry chicks, I asked myself "what if each crumb is a planet, just like planet Earth, where sorrowful or cheerful lives of conscious beings are unraveling?" And I considered whether our planet, together with all the stars we saw at night, which seemed so far away, were nothing but mere crumbs in a giant's pocket, who in turn was himself living on a planet which was nothing but a crumb in a another giant's pocket, and so on…

Of course one cannot truly conceive of this theoretical concept, which could repeat endlessly, without getting a headache. I don't consider myself a mystic, nor am I a person with expertise in quantum physics, but from what I've read, to this day scientists are trying ardently to understand, at least conceptually, the expansion of the universe and to agree on the smallest existent particle of matter.

Back then, at the age of six, I asked myself for the first time, intuitively, without words, if I "destroyed universes" when I fed the chickens the leftover breadcrumbs, and if we, too, will find our end swallowed by "giants"—or giant forces, dematerializing in an incomprehensible darkness... And what is my connection with those spaces, my mission in these micro and macro universes?

CF: *Do you believe that we have access to that information, or that we can grasp a smidgen of it by being around those who can penetrate those scientific mysteries?*

SM: Perhaps... I remember how, across the street from where my grandparents were living, in Tohanul Vechi, a small village at the foot of the Carpathian Mountains, lived the son of the local elementary teacher, who had recently been accepted, near the top of the list, to the Faculty of Physics, University of Bucharest, and who, over time, ended up teaching at the Brookhaven National Laboratory, Yale University and chairing the European Physical Society's Nuclear Physics Division. Who knows what I picked up from half-heard conversations taking place on the topics of physics and the mysteries of the universe while my grandmother was serving him cherry preserve and I was pedaling zealously on my tricycle? Or perhaps there was an osmosis taking place, as I knew that he was "cramming" vast amounts of material before the entrance exams ... perhaps subtle and overly simplified paradigms were being transferred in the ether of that simple street in that humble village, and we were all partaking in it .... An involuntary, anecdotal memory, an amusing, improbable thought, which however I couldn't abstain from sharing.

CF: *Let me come back to an earlier question, one that provoked both of us to expand a dialogue that started as a casual exchange into an ampler discussion. What are we doing here on Earth?*

SM: I believe that our souls have yearned to have an experience on this planet, an active participation in a physical life. We are spiritual beings having a human experience (and not the other way around), an experience that offers us an opportunity to learn, to heal, to elevate ourselves, and hopefully our peers, through the act of giving and receiving love. We are part of that universal energy which connects us with divinity.

If we are to accept this point of view, I believe there is a continuum where at one end we have the incarnation of avatars such as Jesus, Buddha, Vishnu and everything they represent: tolerance, truth, love, light, a complete union with Divine Consciousness; at the other end we have that which is embodied by destruction, annihilation, extermination, racism, subjugation, abuse, separation, etc. Perhaps all we can do, we, the "small waves," is to lean toward that 51% on the continuum, to lean toward the light. And here, I can't abstain from mentioning that aura which each person is exuding, and in which, it is said, there are no secrets, where all our deeds and thoughts, all our sufferings and joys are mirrored in our eyes and emanate in the energy that surrounds us and which we project into the world, like invisible, sparkly neon signs. Becoming conscious of which end of the axis we lean towards is of paramount importance.

CF: *How do we aim toward the luminous part of the axis? Practically, what do we have to do?*

SM: I'd like to choose an aspect of my life which receives a great deal of my effort and energy, namely the organization I founded and run: Blue Heron Foundation. Those who know me, know that I try to bring to life, to the best of my abilities, and with the help of a remarkable team, the mission of a dream project. This project is the fruit of a conscious intention: improving the quality of life of Romanian and Moldovan abandoned youth and offering them greater opportunities by awarding them college scholarships.

More specifically, we cover not only their college tuition in Romania, but we also pay for additional courses such as English, computer literacy, driving lessons, etc. Furthermore, we pair each student with a mentor from their chosen field who is established enough to give guidance, encouragement and support. Every year we have approximately 100 students in our program (of whom about 10% are in medical school!), youngsters who come from approximately 25 of Romania's 40 regions. In exchange for the help given to them, we require that they receive passing grades on all their exams, perform 5 hours of volunteer work every week and write a monthly report, which they submit to us and to their mentors; this report describes not only their struggles but also their successes and gratitude for anything they consider to be a gift in their lives. In fact, what we are doing is helping them understand their own inner world in a broader and more profound way. Through the volunteer work they perform, they not only gain experience and cultivate the qualities of selflessness and altruism, they also experience the joy and increased self-assurance that comes with the uplifting of an individual or society. Recently, we have expanded to the Republic of Moldova, the country with the highest rate of human trafficking in Europe (sexual and labor exploitation, as well as organ trafficking). It may seem like a small wave, but we know, after listening to the students' testimonies and witnessing their successes, that we have changed destinies, that we have interrupted a cycle of poverty and abandonment and that this will positively affect generations to come... It's quite possible that the children and grandchildren of these youngsters will also reap the fruit of these apparently small but positive efforts.

CF: *Are you also trying to uplift the spiritual level of the Blue Heron Foundation's scholarship recipients?*

SM: Most definitely. It is an element of the program carefully conceived and integrated, particularly within the mentorship program. The questions they have to answer in their monthly journals and the way in which our psychologists and social workers monitor this program, incorporate a philosophy aligned with the foundation's mission and the vision I have as the founder. We stress the notion that we reject hierarchies, that we believe we're all guests of equal importance on this planet, that life is a gift we must be grateful for and allow to blossom. Moreover, we accentuate the indisputable value we see inherent in each one of them and communicate to them the courage of seeing themselves in the same manner. We continuously express our respect for the strength they demonstrate in surmounting unimaginable suffering and their ability to create a new and positive trajectory in spite of past traumas.

If we observe where they started out and where they are now, it is indeed hard to imagine what they've overcome to get where they are...a lesson for the majority of us who have grown up with adequate love and material and emotional stability, with positive role models and sensible moral values. We respect their religious practices and at the same time we remind them that our donors belong to various belief systems, including agnosticism and atheism. Our intention is to help guide them, through deeds and the way they see the world and themselves, toward those points on the axis where truth, love, forgiveness and hope reside. I would also add that spirituality—that essence of all religions—resides in the same place.

What I described above is one of the many ways through which we can elevate ourselves and our fellow human beings. I believe that there are many different deeds that can surpass the efforts of a philanthropic organization. A biologist who makes a discovery that saves many lives, a professor who helps a student to believe in himself, a poet whose metaphor helps us see a parent unjustly judged in a new light, are just a few examples of the energy of high consciousness manifested in our tangible universe.

But for me, I have to confess, nothing is more wondrous and seductive than being the creator of great deeds, at first sight committed only in ether. What can hold more power than creating, with that magic wand of the White Magician, quiet acts of great power brought into being through love and optimism, through thoughts, prayers, intentions, visualizations?

Can We Choose Our Destiny?

> "When you don't dream your life, you have to settle
> for the nightmare being dreamed by others."
> "There are two kinds of people in the world: those who
> are dreamers and those who are being dreamed."
> —Alberto Villoldo

CF: *Why did you choose to study spiritual psychology?*

SM: I could say it was sheer coincidence, yet I believe nothing is mere accident. The opportunity encountered was perhaps pure synchronicity, yet my decision to take advantage of it was a conscious choice.

I was working in a private wellness clinic in Los Angeles in 1991, more specifically within their stress management program. On various occasions, I would venture into pertinent conversations with my supervisor, and after delving into topics such as the most obvious factors influencing our stress level—daily tensions, anxieties, the way in which we communicate and relax, how we handle a crisis situation—we'd arrive at more esoteric subjects: prayer, meditation, spirituality…that something that can only be identified with our sixth sense. He was also the one who mentioned the master's degree in applied spiritual psychology at University of Santa Monica. Within a short time I enrolled in the school. Looking back, I realize that every single hour spent in that program felt like a deep immersion in a world I had always known it existed, a world I was hungry to explore and talk openly about, but which no professional or accredited institution had adopted as part of their curriculum, at least not up to that moment. I realized how deeply hungry I had been for such information, and how deeply aligned those subjects were with my inner questions and restless searches.

Because of that program, I have fine-tuned another way of viewing psychology, "the study of mind and behavior" (really, the experience of life), through a lens that is attuned to Spirit. Because of that, a couple of years later, when I was accepted into the doctoral program at the California School of Professional Psychology, I realized I needed more beyond the purely scientific way, which described psychology as being strictly a science of the mind, emotions and behavior. Approaching psychology as simply a science based on research and empirical observation is at the very least incomplete, as it excludes the very etymology of the word. "Psyche" after all means "soul, life, breath." Have we all forgotten about Psyche, the mortal princess who became Eros's wife and the Goddess of the Soul?

Before completing the first year of the doctorate, I left the program. It wasn't easy, as I am a person who finds the esthetic symmetry in completing arches of endeavors very satisfying. However, I never regretted it. I felt I had honored my heart, knowing that I would have invested a big chunk of my time (at least five years) pursuing a program that did not deeply resonate with me.

Since then, I've become highly conscious of the effort I've always made to balance two worlds: the "tangible" material world that unfolds according to accepted and observed laws and rules, and the world of non-conformity, undefeated by rigid societal norms or by paradigms filtered purely through critical thinking, paradigms that would have clipped my wings and my need to dream, to understand and reinvent myself permanently.

Maintaining my equilibrium on that very narrow balance beam continued, and since then I have dedicated myself to being an eternal student of life, committed to the study of psychology, esoteric studies, mythology and spirituality, whether through readings, attending workshops or traveling, in an effort to learn and understand the paths that get us "up there," in the realms where time and space cease to exist. To my great fascination, I have found that in spite of the wildly disparate religious or spiritual practices people may engage in at different ends of the world, there are common denominators of how we connect with Spirit, the Higher Power, Higher Order (whatever one wants to call it). It is important not to get lost in the method; after all, no one wants to be a professional meditator, people want to be free.

CF: *Are religious or spiritual practices the only ways to get to that higher realm beyond time and space?*

SM: The simple discipline of daily meditation or the regular recital of catechisms does not guarantee that we necessarily get there. And most certainly, if we do get to that place, like all states, it's temporary. The ultimate test may be the ability to bring back to our daily lives the memory of the experience of divinity. I often think that the greater challenge is reserved for us—ordinary people with families, jobs and many worldly responsibilities, forced to survive in a world imbued with alienation, competition, materialism, vices—than for the monks and nuns isolated in monasteries, sunk solely in sacred teachings and rituals. The idea is to give ourselves wholeheartedly to all we do, and yet, to not become so narrow in focus as to forget who we are beyond our transitory lives.

CF: *Are there mentors or encounters which helped you discover yourself or which have influenced you in this adventure of spiritual awakening?*

SM: Not to contradict myself, on the contrary, to underline my point of view, I'd like to bring up a long-term experience I had in the bosom of a psychotherapeutic approach so widely accepted in the West: psychoanalysis. Between 1993 and 1998 I had the welcome opportunity to be analyzed, three times a week, by a very respected psychiatrist in the Los Angeles area. Harvard educated with extensive experience in his specialty, Dr. R's method was deeply rooted in the works of Sigmund Freud, Otto Rank and Donald Winnicott, yet blended with his classic psychoanalytic methods, there was an incredibly warm and humanistic leitmotif punctuating his approach. I must confess we often clashed heads with regards to my "spiritual" filter of the world (the term "spiritual" in itself I believe irritated him) and his rather conventional way of filtering "reality." We did however find common ground, our own private Switzerland that bridged spirituality and clinical psychology, in analyzing dreams and the subconscious. And I do remember well my feelings toward him, beyond the semantics which transpired between us: he was a man of intentions immaculate and clear, determined to deeply understand my thinking process and all that was a misidentification, a judgment, an "untruth," resolute in his approach to help me heal and liberate myself.

The "healing" (rather, an experience which helped me transform and step onto the next level of consciousness) that unfolded inside of me, took place because I felt he genuinely valued me as a human being, believed in me and my ability to manifest my highest potential; it was transferred to me through the energy that lay behind his words. If this non-verbal transfer, which affected my inner being in a positive and deep way, would not have taken place, none of his Harvard diplomas, logical or sophisticated psychoanalytical explanations about my personality or my subconscious, would have impacted me. They would have, most likely, had minimal value or perhaps affected me negatively.

At University of Santa Monica, where in 1993 I received my Masters in Applied Spiritual Psychology, I studied with doctors Ron and Mary Hulnick, who were not only the President and Academic Vice President but also international innovators in the field of spiritual psychology. They had received their doctorate degrees in psychology and completed their internships at traditional accredited universities, yet, like a select group of other psychologists who felt that the traditional approaches failed to provide deep and lasting healing, they embarked on the path of delving deeper into the nature of the human soul. The program they developed at University of Santa Monica taught us how to do that not only by reading material that questioned the templates of our lives, but most often through experiential, applied learning, which, I believe, beats any theory, as it gives us the opportunity to see tangible results. Those were certainly intense years, a time when I challenged many of the paradigms I was inhabiting. In retrospect, I am absolutely sure that remarkable, kind, accomplished Dr. R and heart-and soul-centered Ron and Mary Hulnick were not only my teachers and therapists but spiritual guides I was meant to have in this lifetime.

CF: *Do you believe in destiny? How would you define it?*

SM: I believe we each have certain missions to accomplish in this lifetime. As years passed, I learned to listen more carefully to my inner voice, to what exactly animates my interior (anima means "soul," but also "spirit"). I believe that in life we encounter people and situations that represent definite signs and opportunities in our existential trajectory. When you become "animated" it means you are moved, stirred, affected by something or someone. It is a sign that we must pay close attention and consider the opportunity that is presented to us; it is an invitation to explore something, to avoid something or to risk a new path in life.

In addition, we come into the world with so called genetic gifts and aptitudes, ultimately all originating from "that" place where consciousness resides, in that invisible, mysterious "dark matter" which physicists are still struggling to understand and demonstrate. Along the path, we meet people who evoke in us an immediate, instinctive attraction, and it becomes clear that we are meant to share the road for a while. A child may be born with certain talents which may attract the attention of those around him, but later on, his successful manifestation depends on the environmental backdrop against which those talents can be cultivated … or not.

CF: *How unforgiving is destiny?*

SM: There are certain unavoidable elements that we encounter on our life's trajectory: from the country and family in which we are born, to the genetic material we inherit which contours our physical attributes, to the talents and the type of intelligence that have been passed on to us, all the way to inevitable tragedies. While these elements are immutable on our trajectory, I do believe in the great gift that has been bestowed on all of us: *the ability to choose how we interpret what unfolds.*

The confidence we have in our inherited traits, what we choose to do not only with the talents but also with the weaknesses that were passed on to us, the strength we demonstrate in the face of tragedies, the ability to view breakdowns as opportunities to become wiser and stronger in our hearts rather than classifying them as permanent failures … all these can shape a destiny.

CF: *Can we choose our destiny? Can we change it? And if so, when and how?*

SM: Personally, I have come to understand why certain doors were shut in my face over the years, no matter how hard I tried, no matter how hard I wanted to continue in a certain direction (gymnastics, certain intimate relationships, my PhD). I am thoroughly convinced that they were not part of my "curriculum" and it was important to accept and resolve those stunted paths inside myself. I see clearly, looking behind, a divine harmony in the trajectory I traveled, and I believe I have a deep understanding about why certain dreams didn't come to pass.

I also spoke earlier about the incredible importance of intentions—and by "intentions" I am referring to conscious choices not only at life's grand crossroads but also at its minor junctions. Through the smaller—even daily—choices, as well as through a profound and constant attention to that which animates our interior, we can truly be active agents in shaping a destiny... but we don't create it in its entirety. In the end, destiny is perhaps a conscious co-creation between us and Divinity.

In the world of spiritual psychology there are two notions believed to play a fundamental role in life's trajectory: "sacred contracts," those pacts we supposedly close with Spirit before we are born, and karma, the totality of the thoughts, words and deeds we accumulate over time[3].

One of the stories that is still engraved in my mind is a Hindu tale about a yogi and his disciple. It is said that this yogi master had the ability to heal people suffering from myriad maladies on the spot, so people were flocking from all corners to be touched by his healing hands. One day, a lamenting mother brought

---

[3] The term itself need have no exclusive connection to any particular faith tradition.

her sick child to the yogi; she was sobbing and begging for a miracle. The master ignored her completely and asked her curtly to leave the place. The disciple could not believe his master's reaction. He, who had brought instant recovery to so many seekers, why and how could he have allowed himself to be so ruthless and cold?

The Yogi responded: "I did not try to heal them because, when they approached me, I saw beyond the now, into their past lives: the mother had been a ruthless judge, her son the executioner, carrying out her cold-blooded terminal orders. This lifetime was meant to be spent in suffering, an opportunity to feel the pain of injustice and lack of compassion. I'm not meddling with that."

Alienation.
Animism & Shamanism.

CF: *In recent dialogues, we spoke about animism and shamanism, currents which you confessed had stirred your interest. Could animism, understood in a refined fashion that goes beyond a basic belief in the force of the spirits, represent a path to salvation?*

SM: Animism, the way it is used in shamanism, considers that not only human beings, but other entities as well—like animals or plants—possess a soul and are "agents with a consciousness." For an animist adept, nothing is a chance occurrence, no event is an accident; they all have personal implications. A dog may be "friendly," a tree may be "wise," a sky may be "happy," a certain landscape "dangerous."

CF: *We live in a world of glass and concrete, digitized, so often removed from the blue sky, the wind's whisper, the smell of the grass, of animals' breath. We've broken off from the ancestral universe.*

We are increasingly more efficient, multitaskers with impressive technical abilities, and slaves to comfort. Could the departure from nature and our alienation in our modern world, in particular in the big cities, be the price of civilization?

SM: Most recently there has been a great deal written about neo-shamanism, a newer current which encompasses beliefs and practices of communication with the spiritual world, and about the connection between alienation (that distinctive characteristic of lives in the Western world) and *animism*, where alienation does not exist. Neo-shamanism supports the notion that alienation, when we feel that life lacks meaning, that we don't belong in the world, is not an inevitable condition of our modern civilization.

CF: *The pessimists support the notion that the only way to return to nature is through a catastrophe…*

SM: I deeply hope it won't be through catastrophe, but through an "awakening" of our spiritual nature, an awakening that is birthed from within. I think often of alienation when I drive in Los Angeles—and I drive a minimum of four hours daily—alone, on its sprawling streets, with deserted sidewalks where pedestrians are a rare sight, and where we are each isolated in our individual vehicle. I think of it also when I attend events where, at the end, I almost always feel emptier on the inside than when I first arrived; when I see children corrupted by hours of non-stop video games, the opportunity for spontaneous playing in nature or on neighborhood streets vanished; or when I change the TV channel unmoved by the wounded people in Afghanistan or the dead in Syria. I wonder if it is just a coincidence that JRR Tolkien's *Lord of the Rings* is the favorite book of the 21st century, with its sentient beings, horses, eagles, trees, mountains and animated landscapes.

I have the belief that more and more of us will discover and reside in that "Higher Self," the "Superior Self" that exists inside all of us, with its guiding light and magic, and that we will have a deeper understanding of our origin and belonging, and our place in the divine constellation.

CF: *If in the olden days, in Romania, the term alienation was associated mainly with psychiatric conditions, today it has become a common term, used most often to define loneliness, the absence of emotions and the effect of stress on certain vulnerable temperaments. Alienation haunts not only the typical American, but the uprooted immigrant as well. Have you ever felt you were preyed upon by alienation, the way it is perceived in today's times?*

SM: Of course. As immigrants, the fear of falling into the precipice of alienation haunts us intensely, and we search feverishly for pillars of light that can anchor us more solidly in our new reality.

CF: *How can you oppose alienation in an alienated world?*

SM: I notice it all around me, for example in the simple desire to not separate myself from reference points which anchor me in a more awakened existence, such as my resistance to online banking... I end up choosing to drive to the bank so that I can have a face to face experience with the bank employee. The fact that the same Armenian bank officer has been helping me for over a dozen years and that she wasn't yet transferred to a new branch—a rarity these days—has heightened my experience of being in the world in a way the computer could never replace.

Recently I heard an interview on NPR about carpooling.com, a program which encourages local rideshares and which seems to be gaining in popularity. I listened to testimonials that pointed to the riders' joy in encountering new people, new stories, new ways of seeing the world, through the opportunity of this experience. One person shared his touching story of meeting his significant other in this way... As I ponder more deeply about it, I am thinking that alienation may also mean the lack of opportunity to penetrate the nature of the world in greater depth, that bottom of the interior ocean which can only be touched when we are immersed in the reading of a book of great artistic value, or when we have a deep and sincere conversation with a friend.

If we are not aware, we can be swept way too often and easily into the enticing vortex of social media, where the brain, let's be honest, the majority of time is engaged in a fairly superficial way, not in a way that deeply nourishes our being. On the same day and on the same NPR program, perhaps not by pure chance, a neurologist was talking about the neurons which fire up and stimulate other like neurons: the more we excite the neurons that require minimal concentration (or those that need to shift to varying points of interest), the more we develop those particular kinds of neurons and lose the ability to concentrate for long periods of time. That which deeply nourishes our interior expands beyond the border of a striking photograph or quote, those dazzling modes of expression that inundate our senses and which can hold us captive in the superficial waters of our consciousness.

But sometimes I also ask myself: what if we allow ourselves to be carried away by the wave of this alienation? Would we become better adapted, as in the survival of the fittest? Would those individuals be more equipped to make it in the competitive dynamic of the global world we live in?

I still believe that it's in our power to stand for a richer, more nuanced existence, a more profoundly human existence where our six senses—sight, taste, hearing, touch, smell but also INTUITION—are engaged in our living as much as possible.

Those following the thread of spirituality often believe that being incarnated on Terra is a divine gift, not easily bequeathed to yearning souls… If we were to embrace this notion, wouldn't we have to live life as fully and as wholeheartedly as possible?

Religion. Dogma. Divinity.

CF: *Is religion the only path to divinity?*

SM: Even though I grew up in a country where religion was overtly discouraged and parents seemed to have no opinion about God whatsoever, everything on my path from childhood all the way to this moment in my life has been punctuated by opportunities to question and delve into the possibility of weaving divinity into my life. It so happened that my maternal grandfather was a priest and archdeacon in the prevalent religion of the country, Romanian Orthodoxy, and my paternal grandmother was a remarkably pious woman with an uncanny intuition and attachment to age old religious rituals; my aunt—also a big presence in my life—was an artist who renovated and painted Byzantine churches. During my teens, my family immigrated to Salt Lake City and I lived among Mormons for eight years, forging heartfelt relationships with many co-workers, witnessing on a regular basis the great role religion played in their lives. In my early twenties, I completed a master's degree in spiritual psychology and soon after I married into a Jewish

Los Angeles family where, even though every member had very much identified with the cultural aspect of being Jewish, my mother-in-law was the only practitioner of a religion … and that was Zen Buddhism. These experiences were more than enough to instill in me a deep respect and tolerance for all paths, knowing full well that there isn't just one road.

Moreover, I am an avid reader of works on the subject and I have heartfelt conversations with friends of Christian, Muslim, Kabbalah and Hindu faiths. What I often look for in our conversations is finding the common denominators that exist not only in religions, but also in revelations that unfold while meditating, while in nature, while creating a work of art, or making a meaningful discovery. The above-described experiences guided me towards believing that there is an ethereal thread that connects all these paths and which carries us closer to that divine matrix. I do however believe that it is not guaranteed that through a religion we can touch the divine, the traps being dogma and fanaticism.

In order to evoke a clearer image of these concepts, one would have to imagine a journey from Los Angeles to New York. In order to get there, we can go by plane, bus, hot air balloon, bicycle, walk, etc. Many may end up arguing over the best method, insisting that their way is the only right way or the best way, forgetting that the intention is a simple one: to get to New York. The same unfolds when our destination is Divinity. I've always held back from hierarchizing religions…it's almost as if asking a mother to tell you who her favorite child is.

CF: *Do we need intermediaries in our relationship with divinity? Have you been marked by any events experienced in a holy abode?*

SM: I remember an incident that took place in 2009. I was in Suceava where, since 2005, Blue Heron Foundation, the organization I run, pays for the college tuition and offers emotional support to dozens of orphaned and abandoned young men and women who attend university. There we have a partnership with a non-governmental organization led by a very dynamic lady, someone who possesses endless energy not only for her projects, but also for her very active spiritual life. She suggested a visit to the oldest church in Suceava, where, she said, "almost every prayer is answered."

Being a big fan of miracles of all kinds, before meeting with the students, I decided to make a quick stop at St. Gheorghe Church (also known as the "Mirauti Church," built in the 14th century). I arrived there during a rainy afternoon and was told that the procedure was simply to write the names of our loved ones on a piece of paper and hand it to the monk, along with a donation. It was quite different than what I had imagined, but thought "what do I have to lose?"

and wrote the names of all those dear to me on the list, making sure to add "and all the students in the Blue Heron Program."

With a $20 bill, I headed toward the monk who was sitting in an alcove, collecting the lists and the money that came with them, most of them humble donations from humble people. I came face to face with him, and shortly after scanning the paper I noticed he turned red and I could gather from his nonverbal gestures that something was amiss. The young monk, no older than 35, was turning red and frowning as he was going down the list reading the "exotic" names I had written down; he finally gave off a big sigh which seemed to come from a very deep place inside, and in a distressed and troubled tone he asked me "so and so, and so and so (all English names), who are they?"

Even though it seemed like a very natural question, there was no doubt in my mind that there was anxiety and nervousness inside of him, that he was off his axis, so to speak, and I felt he had passed on to me that suspenseful restlessness. I answered back, making a great effort to keep a natural tone: "My husband, my sons, nephews, relatives…"

"I seeee…and where do they live?"

"The majority of them live in the United States."

From that moment on I understood where the interrogation was heading and felt that the little old church started spinning with me in it. I had a firm feeling that he was experiencing something similar, but continued to question me: "Did you have a religious ceremony when you got married?"

"Yes." At this moment the redness in his face intensified. "And is your husband Romanian?"

"No."

The stuffy air and the dampness of the old church in dire need of renovation all of a sudden came into my awareness, and I felt as if I were about to choke. "And who officiated the religious ceremony?"

"A Buddhist Rabbi." At that point I sensed an internal collapse unfolding in his head and body. It was so strong that I had to look up to ensure the ceiling wasn't falling on us.

But he came back to his senses enough to tell me "Ah, you amputated your soul!", words which instantly woke me up to another level of awareness and anguish: "I didn't marry my husband for his religion, but for who he is, as a person," and quickly, inside of me I uttered "please God, forgive him, as he doesn't know what he is saying," only to hear him enunciate the same thoughts out loud "may her sins be lifted as she knows not what she is saying."

Awoken from the reverie of the last minutes— minutes which had a completely different sense of time—I found my voice and said "before my Romanian Orthodox priest grandfather died" (at this point his eyes bulged out of the orbits and the redness in his face started changing shades), "before he died, he knew I was about to marry someone of a different faith, and he conducted an intimate ceremony, just for the two of us, blessing the union." I pronounced these words serenely and felt uplifted by the dusty memory that had popped up in my mind.

He took a deep breath and, gloomily, he lifted his eyes toward the sky: "Up there in heaven, your grandfather will then carry the burden of your sin."

I said: "I have the feeling that you've spread enough negative energy for now, I want my list back please. And you can keep the money earned by my husband." He returned the piece of paper, kept the $20 from my Jewish husband, and I retired to a secluded corner of the church to pray, convinced once again that there isn't necessarily a need for intermediaries.

The following day I was already in Iasi, the capital of Moldova in the olden times, ready for a get together with yet another group of our students. Still, not feeling completely over what had happened in the Mirauti Church, I decided to take a stroll, to clear my head before meeting our students. During the walk, I was secretly hoping to find some antiquarians with long forgotten treasures and came across a modern day bookstore with an intriguing display of thought provoking titles in the window. My eyes fell on the recently published *About the Beautiful Man* by Dan Puric, an author I had remembered reading several years prior. Since his earlier essays on themes about women and love had captivated me, I decided to take a chance on his new book.

During that very same evening, after the meeting with our scholarship recipients, I settled in the comfortable bed at the Ecumenical Institute Motel (a humble but exceptionally clean place I always end up staying when I visit Iasi), and eagerly started reading the book. I so needed to rebuild myself. I started reading, but after just a few pages, the feeling of anticipated upliftment had disappeared. Somehow, the voice channeled by that monk was present again on the pages of this author—who was not only a writer, but also an actor, pantomime and Orthodox apologist. My mind was suddenly flooded with the voices of the Mormon apologists, and then the Muslim ones too, all these devotees who had the same stern beliefs that the only true path is that which *they* see and are embarked on, the path they support and defend with "supportive evidence" of historical facts, quotes from legitimate but secret documents, where the "only" and the "real" truth lies, documents found after tireless quests and so quietly guarded in holy sanctuaries.

The problem, as it appears to me is: to which religion does this exclusive club belong? I thought about how certain religions are a perfect fit for certain cultures and countries, and I belong to the opinion that for many people, those paths are the best ways *for them* to connect with the Divine. But, when DOGMA and

FANATICISM appear, we need not look further than our contemporary history to see the destructive, catastrophic consequences that ensue when one chooses the narrow path. What happened on September 11, 2001 is only one of the many testaments … history is riddled with them.

For almost two years I decided to not share with my husband what had transpired in that church. I told myself "he's only visited Romania once. Why should I negatively influence his already precarious opinion about my homeland; why shatter the possibility of a positive view about this country and the Romanian people?" The sad thing was that I hadn't yet thoroughly processed what had happened in that church and was still carrying with me the bitter taste of the episode, along with a restless yearning to let it all out. I expected perhaps explosive reactions, or even worse, deep and quiet ones suffused with sadness and sorrow, mirroring the despondency I had experienced during the past two years. I was surprised by his matter-of-factness, by how little the occurrence I had just shared affected him: "He is a simple man, with narrow views, why would you, even for a moment, let it get to you?" And immediately, the commentary of a good friend, originally from Ethiopia and educated at Princeton, popped into my mind. I had asked her if she ever felt treated differently in her life based on the color of her skin. She too, had responded with quite a *je m'en fiche* air. "Probably, but it's not my issue, it's their lesson, their growth path. My only responsibility is not to get caught."

CF: *We hear that when a divine miracle happens, there is just as much "magic" as there is autosuggestion. Do you believe in the miracle of the prayer?*

SM: Generally yes. But since a very young age, I had the intuition to add, "If it is for my or our highest good" at the end of each prayer.

I have vivid memories when, at the age of 14, I'd go to church by myself. There was this secluded little church on Mayakovski Street in Brasov that I'd go to; I would get on my knees and pray to receive the government's approval to come to America. However, as anxious as I was to have my prayers answered, I was just as aware that I couldn't blindly beg for something, because, I asked myself, "What if the plane crashes? Or what if a bigger drama is awaiting us across the ocean?"

Later on, when I was working on my Masters in Applied Spiritual Psychology, we learned about the importance of adding at the end of every prayer "for the highest good of all concerned," the reason being the existence of a superior order, which not only affects us, but the entire world. Being "small" and incapable of having this panoramic perspective, we need to possess sufficient humility to pray in such a way that our prayer will be received and integrated into the harmony of the greater macrocosm.

CF: *What happens if our prayer is not answered?*

SM: When, for example, the end of an era descends upon us, or a life is prematurely taken, when a certain door is not meant to open or a certain wish not meant to come true, I do believe that that is how it's meant to be, and we have to know to accept the outcome and believe in a higher order, even if, from our narrow perspective, we are incapable of seeing. Many yogis believe that only half of our world falls under the laws of logic; the rest is pure faith.

When we pray to the orders of the Divine, it is important to not only ask for things "give me this, make this happen," but to also use this opportunity to demonstrate our gratitude for the immensity of the "simple" gifts received from life: from the joy of feeling the sun's rays on our skin, to the miracle of having a heart which moment by moment does its job, pulsating in our chest, from the secret meanings that have been revealed to us, to the dreams we've transformed into reality or the peace we've attained through forgiveness…We have endless reasons to be thankful and grateful.

CF: *But a prayer that hasn't been answered, isn't it, after all, a defeat?*

SM: From the experiences I acquired during my master's degree (where, over the two years, I listened to hundreds of "sharings" from my fellow students), I understood that a great many of us pray for things in our lives to be different than they are. Even though it is totally normal to want to change things that are a source of pain or things that don't seem aligned with a desired life trajectory, it is of paramount importance to weigh what needs to be accepted and what truly needs to be changed. The ability and the wisdom to know which situations or limits have to be accepted, things that ultimately cannot or should not be dispersed of or shuffled around, can bring us a great deal of inner peace.

CF: *Is the prayer—or imploration—done in extreme need, from a place of suffering or terror, stronger than the daily ritual? Is divinity more "impressed" by our desperation?*

SM: I hope it doesn't sound vulgar, but I often think of the totality of our prayers as if it were a bank account. I believe it is important to add daily "payments" so that in time of real need, we feel more strengthened by our accumulated "deposits." I believe it's important to pray or send light, on a regular basis, to ourselves and to those we love. I've learned from those who know a great deal about prayer, to also send light and ask for resolve for those people and situations which create misunderstandings or are a source of suffering in our lives, our so called "enemies." I've also heard it said over and over, that nothing is more powerful than the prayer of a parent or grandparent. To this day I remember my grandmother praying for my sister and me. She used to tell us she was praying for our future, so that, when she made her passage to the other realm, we'd still be protected and guided by the light.

Since then, my sister and I have been through a great deal, but we've always felt protected and guided by those invisible ascended masters, teachers of light and that "team of angels" our grandmother had summoned for our protection since we were little girls. On a more earthly note, she also accumulated traditional Romanian quilts and high quality monogrammed bedding for our dowry. The "trousseau" ended up scattered to the four winds, but the protective, guiding light continues its hold to this day.

The fact that my sister and I have come to live the so-called "American dream" is just the tip of the iceberg, because the effort that got us there and the way our lives unfold on a daily basis are in fact the result of a great deal of prayer and focused spiritual practice accumulated over many generations.

Sin. Guilt. Punishment.

CF: *Can spiritual education heal us of guilt?*

SM: The notion of guilt has to be explained, because every single action, word or thought we have is neutral until we add a label to it and we judge it as being good, bad, a failure, a triumph etc. Something that may seem relatively normal in our society, may be considered a sin in another, based on religious or political beliefs or based on that society's traditions.

For example, there are many places in the world where, for a man, it is a sin to ever divorce his wife; if he falls in love with another woman, he can marry her, but he is forced to also stay married to the first (or first two or three) as long as he is able to support them in the same lifestyle they've been accustomed to. But in the majority of nations, polygamy is considered a sin and against the law. Beyond such obvious examples, there are myriad others that may be vaguer in our culture, such as the consumption of animal products, which in other religions is considered a sin, justified by the fact that it is for the benefit of man, even though it involves sacrificing a life. If for some divorce is a sin, for others, a sin may be the choice of staying in a marriage for moral, ethical or material reasons once the heart stops blossoming in that relationship.

CF: *Is a sin necessarily a moral transgression?*

SM: It is said that in spirituality there is no morality, a theory I'm still testing daily, as I don't like to accept concepts without trying them out and analyzing the results. The notion is that when our intentions, thoughts and deeds come from a deeply spiritual source, they may be aligned with what is considered moral or they may contradict morality. For example, a duty to help my fellow human beings played only a minor role in the creation of the foundation I run and dedicate myself to daily. The deeper motivation has its origin in a much more profound sentiment, born within my soul: the feeling that this deed is part of my sacred contract on earth, the gift I am meant to leave behind.

CF: *A selfish generosity, if I may call it so, meaning that in the process of helping others you ensure you make yourself happy, spiritually speaking. Allow me to return to the statement that spirituality knows no morality. Perhaps a concrete example would convince us.*

SM: Let's choose for example the relationship between love, morality and spirituality. A close friend met a woman and instantly felt a deep and extraordinary sense of connection, a knowing that she was his heart's mate. He also soon found out that she was married and had a child. Within weeks, the mutual sentiment that they belonged to one another was so strong that they made the difficult and drastic decision to "reconfigure" their lives. Since then, 25 years have passed. They are still together; one of the few couples I admire and whose marriage is a source of inspiration. Morally speaking, it is easy to point the finger; from a spiritual perspective, I take my hat off to them, for their courage to follow the voice of their hearts and take responsibility for the difficulty and consequences of that decision.

CF: *Can the punishment that follows the "sin" be absolved through confession and prayer?*

SM: Often during the process of reframing[4], or changing the label we put on an action/opinion/way of being, we resolve an interior turmoil and elevate ourselves to the next level, where self-judgment disappears. But, beyond the way in which we view these actions/words/thoughts which we've labeled "sins," expressing that certain something which burdens our consciousness itself belongs to a psychological-spiritual process which leads to healing. It's a first step.

---

[4] In psychology there is a term called reframing, not unlike adding a new frame around the same painting.

There are parameters that, ideally, if they are present, aid this process. Expressing these internal conditions, be it orally or in writing, is of great importance.

Depending on each individual's personality, level of education or belief system, confession can be addressed to a priest, a therapist, an intimate friend, a mentor, or an entrusted journal.

The notion is to reach the point where we become conscious of the act of self-judgment and have the ability, through sheer inner power, or with the help of a priest/therapist/friend to forgive ourselves. The result is a feeling of release as well as an understanding of interior processes which, because they have been subjected to forgiveness, bring us to an equilibrium on the soul level. Very often, those released from the heaviness that burdened them find their solutions on their own. This is one of the essential elements learned in the program of applied spiritual psychology and has been confirmed to me by dozens and dozens of direct observations made as a student, during which time we took turns in the roles of counselor, client and neutral observer.

CF: *Is Christianity markedly different from Hinduism and Buddhism in the way they approach the notions of sin and punishment?*

SM: In Buddhism the concept of sin doesn't play the kind of central role it has played in Christianity.

There is the notion of "precepts," which are actions, modes of thinking which guide us toward a higher path, a more tolerant and kind one: to not kill another life, to only take what has been offered to you, to tell the truth, to cultivate sexual behavior which protects and deepens the integrity of individuals, families, society. Those who follow Buddhism are encouraged to deepen their understanding of and commitment to these precepts, focusing on that which elevates us on life's axis.

Similarly, in Hinduism we primarily encounter the notion of "karma;" the belief is that all we do, say or think, we carry with us in life, the same way a horse pulls a wagon behind. An example would be a child who sticks his hand in the fire and gets burned. The action is due to his ignorance, as he doesn't yet know the lethal strength of such a force. When we regularly contemplate our deeds, words and thoughts, we delve into a deeper understanding about their profound consequences and, as such, we can make wiser choices in the present and future.

CF: *Does science contradict or is it in opposition to spiritual thinking?*

SM: Perhaps the best reference would be that of Albert Einstein, whose relationship with God—God as in Divine Order—is elaborately analyzed in Walter Isaacson's biography, *Einstein, His Life and Universe.*

Even though from the age of 12 until the end of his life Einstein refused to engage in any religious ritual, from early on in his childhood he retained a profound reverence for the harmony and beauty of what he identified as "God's mind" and the way this consciousness was expressed through the creation of the universe and its laws.

One of the most well-known stories is that in which, having been invited to a formal dinner, Einstein was provoked by one of the guests to express his opinion about religion. His answer surprised many cynics who were present there: "Try and penetrate with our limited means the secrets of nature and you will find that, behind all the discernible laws and connections, there remains something subtle, intangible and inexplicable. Veneration for this force beyond anything that we can comprehend is my religion. To that extent I am, in fact, religious."

He is also known for his humility in the face of nature's miracles, of which he spoke numerous times: "Everyone who is seriously involved in the pursuit of science becomes convinced that a spirit is manifest in the laws of the Universe—a spirit vastly superior to that of man, and one in the face of which we, with our modest powers, must feel humble."

Einstein considered this cosmic religion the common source of all arts and sciences. Similar to Spinoza, he does not believe in a personal god who interacts directly with man, but a divine order manifested in the laws that dominate the way the universe unfolds. Furthermore, he was of the opinion that scientific discoveries can be interpreted as discoveries related to divine order.

CF: *Can an atheist find a place for himself in the spiritual equation?*

SM: It is interesting how often the most devout atheists are at the same time individuals who understand and have a deep respect for nature, are often fascinated and accomplished in sciences and may have a highly developed moral and ethical sense. I believe that the great contradictions derived from the notions of "religion," "spirituality," "divinity," "cosmic order" are the result of semantic misinterpretations.

When someone proclaims "I don't believe in God" it may mean something as simple as "I don't believe in an old man who floats above the clouds and is interested in our personal destinies." At the same time, the same person may be paying attention to his dreams, to insights which often prove to be prophetic and which he takes into consideration; or he may be attuned to events which may have made his hair stand on end.

Another example would be the notion of "believing in Jesus" versus believing in "Christ Consciousness," that state of being where we are one with God, a concept of spiritual transcendence of the human consciousness. This state of being was channeled by the great avatars and is, in essence, the state people aspire to reach through the practice of religion.

I am of the opinion that it is important to maintain an open and tolerant attitude toward all points of view, whether they belong to the devotees of various religions or atheists. To not maintain this open attitude means to limit ourselves, to close the doors of knowing and to disregard the trajectory and spiritual evolution of every human being.

Fear of Death

CF: *The fear of death pushed people toward religions and amplified their superstitions. At the same time it stimulated philosophical and creation-related ideas, scientific discoveries and a preoccupation with learning—and going beyond—our biological limits, of trying to slow down the deterioration of our physical bodies as well as attempting to decipher the soul's mystery. If death cannot be avoided, at least life can be prolonged. The questions still remain: Is death the ultimate stage of a human being or is there a transition to "something else?" What happens with our soul after physical death?*

SM: Those who believe the death of our physical bodies is the unavoidable and complete finality may answer quite sure of themselves: "I'd have no problem believing in life after death if there were some scientifically documented cases, tangible events which can demonstrate the existence of that realm. I haven't yet met anyone who has been able to produce such proofs."

On the other hand, those who believe that the soul continues its journey and that at the death of the person it leaves behind a body which is no longer serving a temporary personality, may very well be answering: "There are thousands of documented examples of people who have found themselves in a coma or clinical death, who all had similar experiences, namely that of a soul floating over the physical body, being able to analyze their experience on earth." One of the most recent books I read on the subject was "Dying to Be Me," where the author, Anita Moorjani, describes her journey from cancer, to near death, to complete healing. She develops the idea that we are spiritual beings having a human experience and that we all belong to a larger "whole."

I could easily cite many common elements that show up consistently in these types of out of body experiences that could be cited, details recounted not only by patients but also their doctors about the presence of a white light, often the experience of a "tunnel," encounters with "spirits of light" or with loved ones who have previously deceased, a profound awareness of unconditional love, or nonverbal messages received in a telepathic manner. Another common element is that to some who experience clinical death, unfinished business is brought to their attention and clarified if it is necessary to return and heal a relationship or take on a certain mission in the physical world.

Recently I had an experience which confirmed again that these phenomena do happen around us, perhaps more often than we'd like to believe. Someone very close to our family who considers himself an atheist and does not believe in "life after death," had to photograph an American veteran who had been atrociously disfigured, the victim of an explosion while serving in the Iraq war. Before the actual photo session, they had breakfast together in an attempt to create a more relaxed and natural atmosphere during the photo shoot.

The veteran shared what had happened: the tank he was riding in along with four other soldiers ran over a buried bomb and, after the explosion, he was the only survivor, his face all burned up, unable to ever close his eyelids, skin on his scalp surgically trans-ferred from his stomach, missing his left arm … He related how before the accident he had had no beliefs about life after death, but how, after his experience while in a coma, he began to contemplate deeply his notions about life and death. While in a coma, which had lasted about a week, he went through a number of mystical experiences, where he was floating on an iceberg during the night, guided by the stars, arriv-ing at the understanding in a deep, intuitive way that the time to leave his physical body had not yet come. Today he is one of the most enthusiastic inspirational speakers for wounded veterans. These soldiers have to fight many battles even after they return from war; depression and work reintegration are among their toughest challenges.

CF: *The Egyptian Book of the Dead and The Tibetan Book of the Dead discuss the various stages the soul encounters once it leaves the body. In folk tales the elixir of life without death is a leitmotif. In Islam, the virtuous ones ascend to paradise. In Christianity, there is the hope of afterlife and of resurrection. Belief in the eventual coming of the messiah is a basic and fundamental part of traditional Judaism. Buddhism and Hinduism bring forth the hypothesis of many recurring lives, with the goal of cleansing one's karma: death follows life and another life follows death, unresolved karma (or sins) follow the individual from one life to the next; some can be absolved, others deepen… Reincarnation occurs as many times as necessary for the Spirit to learn from earthly experiences until all karma is balanced, all sins are absolved and the individual becomes self-actualized. Which of these paths do you most resonate with?*

SM: The notions that relate to incarnation can lead to complex conversations, full of passion, but also of controversy, and I believe they represent some of the most fractious topics of spirituality. Individuals are incited by the notion and their opinions vary greatly from those who readily dismiss it as great foolishness to those—even doctors and professors—who not only believe in it but have built their body of work on a philosophy that incorporates this notion… not to mention the hundreds of millions of Hindus and Buddhists who accept the notion as second nature.

For those who believe in reincarnation, it is important to not fall prey to the belief that they are the victims of the accumulation of negative karma (sins) of a previous lifetime, but to continue incessantly to aspire toward the positive continuum of human potential—and of their personal potential—regardless of what they may believe they are "carrying from a previous lifetime." Moreover, it is perhaps wise for them to familiarize themselves with higher notions that relate to impermanence, such as the Sanskrit concept of Samsara—the never-ending wheel of life, birth, death and rebirth, which, of course, can be interpreted literally or metaphorically. For me personally, this was a concept I contemplated in particular while my husband was in the midst of making the movie *Samsara*, whose production spread over a five-year period and took him (at times with the rest of our family in tow) to over 120 locations in 26 countries.

This concept is also reflected in the Hindu holy scriptures where birth and death are manifestations of Maya, the cosmic illusion, as well as in the teachings of Jesus, according to which a true believer "will never see death" (John 8:51). The message is thus the same: birth and death only make sense in the world of relativity. What is interesting is that people, whether or not they believe in reincarnation, give the same answer to the questions "How would I live life if this was my one and only chance?" and "How would I live my life if it were one of many?"

CF: *Can "objectivity" be part of the answer?*

SM: I recently participated in an event at our kids' school and was talking to two other mothers, one of them a therapist. She was quite proud of having recently ordered ten license plate frames that read, "the more I get to know people, the more I love my dog." She said she was giving one to her husband and asked us if we each wanted one. I admit, the personalized message was rather humorous, but half-seriously I wondered out loud if she was going to lose some of her patients. As for myself, I stated that I subscribe to Will Rogers' saying "I never met a man I didn't like." They both stared at me. "Aha!" the psychologist said, "you are one of them…" and she blinked meaningfully. "You are one of the optimists…"

I hadn't realized until that moment that the two camps were so clearly delineated and that the very act of belonging to one of them would affect our "objectivity" lens. It's very possible that my view about life continuing on another dimension is influenced by my general disposition, which, from an early age, resided at the sunnier end of the temperament spectrum. This, however, does not mean I am not a prudent optimist, an individual often nudged by the questions that relate to our existence and suffering, continuously hungry to understand different points of view as they relate to these themes. I am a person who wants to have the confirmation of the heart and of the sixth sense[5] but also to understand experientially. The evaluation of ideas through experience is the ultimate test to determine the merits of an impression or a concept.

On the other hand, I'm perfectly aware that the meaning of the Will Rogers saying may also encompass the notion that when we deeply know a person, we transcend the imperfect and superficial layers of the personality; we go beyond the ego and recognize a human essence beyond superficial judgment. The saying may also refer even to those we thought we disliked or hated from afar, say those of a different race or religion, whom, upon getting to know intimately, we recognize as having the mutual and profound human essence that unites us, whom we really have nothing against beyond our prejudices.

CF: *Do you believe in the alteration of the human spirit, of which we hear more and more, caused by the deterioration of human values, by the proliferation of negative acts and attitudes, by greed, lies, ambition, betrayal and the obsessive pursuit of money, which seem to dominate our civilization globally?*

SM: I believe this fight about how we use our human potential, our energy, becomes increasingly obvious, quite possibly because of the technological

---

[5] That "other" sense responsible for intuition, the thread that connects us with the reality of our dreams, premonitions, etc.

century we live in, where everything is communicated incredibly fast. In the era of globalization, we've come to discover how small the world really is, how deeply we depend on and influence one another and how, in the age of Youtube, Facebook and Skype, every private living room can become a world stage. We live in a time where we see much more rapidly what the result of an intention/statement/action is, negative or positive. "Instant karma," as it's often called, haunts us around every corner.

If a politician is corrupt or a famous personality is disloyal, the news is available almost instantly in every home. People digest the information; in record time they see the effects and can then look at their own experiences, their own families. The information may very likely make the masses pause; they may look in their own backyard, may ponder for a while on the dramas they are witnessing. They may contemplate the existence of parallels in their lives and then make more moral, ethical or spiritual decisions, which can correct reckless actions.

Equally relevant and obvious are the positive examples of remarkable people. Bill Gates comes to mind, whose innovative genius affected humanity in a positive way and who, besides his contribution to IT and the world economy, has decided to make a profound and long lasting difference through the enormous humanitarian contribution he is gifting the world. Warren Buffett and Paul Allen followed suit.

We cannot not be moved by such trajectories and not feel that these types of people are humanity's hope. The abilities of a single person with a high consciousness can balance out a great deal of negative energy. I want to believe that in this century we will have enough individuals of Mother Teresa's, Mandela's or Bill Gates' caliber, so that the negative intentions and the limited level of consciousness of certain people (those who control the world's nuclear stockpiles come to mind), is outbalanced by those whose minds and souls are filled with light and operate at a high vibration.

CF: *Does your optimism rely as well on the belief that at any moment there is the hope of a spiritual salvation?*

SM: I believe there are models and oases from which we can extract our nourishment. I find them all the time. I believe that the majority of people have the chance of finding the "spiritual tribe" they belong to, even if some of them do it thanks to the internet. And let us not forget that the most important temple resides inside of us and depends on us to cultivate it, to visit it daily and meet daily with our Higher Self or the Holy Spirit, as some may call it. I am convinced that the ability to tilt the balance of humanity toward the Good depends on the innovative and ethical aspects of human potential, guided by high spiritual aspirations.

Feminism and Femininity

CF: *Do you consider yourself a feminist?*

SM: I am not a person who has invested a great deal of energy or effort supporting feminism; however, I am very conscious that not only I, but the majority of my sisters whose lives unfold in the Western society, enjoy the benefits of battles carried during the last century. These struggles were carried out by intelligent, perseverant and courageous women of high consciousness who have fought to obtain, for all of us, rights equal to men's. As is often the case, the interest in a particular topic has not been awakened in me because it happened to be taught in school, but because it showed up haphazardly, in concrete situations when I experienced deep inner constrictions, that whispered in my ear that something was not right, something was not as it naturally should be. I understood during those moments why certain women rolled up their sleeves and initiated the work that demonstrated that, although very different than men, women were actually very much their equals.

CF: *The militant movement of the suffragettes led to tangible legal changes in the United States, and in 1920, women, for the first time, earned the right to vote, civil rights and wage rights equal to a man's. Categorically, a necessary revolution. Do you think that over time, we went from a necessity to an abuse? The exaggerations that followed and which are more and more evident in today's society, including sexual harassment law suits, dramatically transformed a woman's status and modified her outlook. These days, many men perceive women as feared champions. Do you believe that along with the emancipation of women, a paradoxical precipice was formed between the sexes, a competition in which feminism tends to swallow femininity? Is there such a thing as a feminist "machismo?"*

SM: What I observe in the groups that I come in contact with, the American society where my life unfolds, is that, after all the advantages that we enjoy as a result of the aforementioned efforts for equality, somewhere, along the way, a turn was taken that may not necessarily be for a woman's highest good: they only remembered to prove their equality to men, but they forgot that the majority of us are very different than the opposite sex. Women have developed and perfected the qualities which bring the majority of men success in their careers: objectivity, resolution, demonstrative insistence, assertiveness in verbal debate, extensive use of empirical and rational demonstrations, a cerebral approach to issues, even a marked preference for more masculine clothing and footwear. Unfortunately, for many of us, the newly discovered power swallowed up grace, intuition, wisdom, magnetism, sensuality, compassion, the power of silence and gentleness, all those elements which belong to embodying the feminine and femininity.

Personally, in the circles with which I overlap, I feel there is a great crisis of femininity. The qualities mentioned above which describe femininity are disappearing, along with models which embody the "Divine Feminine." Certain psychologists consider that the Divine Feminine[6] may also exist in men, along with those qualities intrinsic to femininity. I personally believe that we need those qualities within our society and families. When both partners exhibit those male characteristics, when the only person maintaining the "feminine flame" is, let's say, a helper from another culture, I believe something is deeply missing. Those feminine qualities don't seem to be in fashion anymore today; they are not encouraged nor appreciated, they are increasingly in danger of extinction. But we need them; we need the energy they emanate.

CF: *What feminine/feminist models do you consider eloquent?*

---

[6] The Divine Feminine is astrologically represented by the Cancer sign.

SM: I identify myself with certain archetypes embodied by Anaïs Nin, who devoted most of her life to the process of understanding herself as a woman, of striving to reach as much as possible, the essence of how the female psyche filters reality. In her journal, she wrote "As I discover myself, I find I am one of many, a symbol. I start understanding the women of now and yesterday. The speechless ones from times past, incoherent, who took refuge behind their speechless intuition, and the ones of today, all action, copies of men. And I, somewhere in between."

Frankly, I also feel I live in my own separate world, my own paradigm, which feels separate from these contemporary quests. I often feel my life is not aligned with the current feminist view, and yet, I want to think that it is an authentic expression of deep contemplation along with an honoring of the intrinsic essence that I came into the world with, beyond the programing of the social/historical/civil views we happen to be surrounded by.

I sometimes fantasize how disappointed Oprah, "the queen of strong and authoritarian women," would be if somehow we'd meet. The way I lead my work as the president of a non-profit is definitely characterized by an authority lined with velvet, a great deal of soul and personal and social relationships of the heart, which I cultivate and lead in what I consider a mainly feminine way. Of course they entail tangible action steps, strategy and organization—not only for fund-raising purposes but also for monitoring the programs we run—yet all springs from a deep yearning to manifest the soul's dream and lead with heart, wisdom, compassion, with grace, gentleness and, yes, beauty.

At home, with my husband, I have a different style. I'm thinking, all of a sudden, of an occurrence that took place during my childhood. I was about nine years old when, along with boys and girls of similar ages, beloved neighbors who were my playmates for many years, I decided to play Indians (like "cowboys and Indians" but without the cowboys). It was clear to me from the beginning what my role was, and I felt totally in my element fulfilling it: I was the one encouraging the men to go and hunt the big bear in the forest and bring it back to the tent, where we were then going to use it for our survival. Of course, feminists would interpret this as a lack of focused energy, capacity, authority and power, but if we all go hunting for bears, who will stay behind to bandage the physical and spiritual wounds of those hurt during the hunt, who will keep the home fires burning, literally and figuratively?

Another example that comes to mind was shared with me by a friend, a distinguished engineering professor at UCLA who has two children and who works side by side with her husband, also a professor.

"Today we took pictures of the nest built by two birds in our garden. We were fascinated to observe how the mother stays in the nest with the chicks, while the father flies to catch food, upon return first feeding his mate, then dividing the remaining food with the chicks."

In parallel, I am haunted by the example of many women who are conscious that they are asked to master both roles and are stretched to the limit, ready to burst at the seams, caring for their family *and* their career; they speak incessantly about exhaustion and are searching for an equilibrium which they seldom find. Their physical appearance reflects this frantic rhythm, in spite of numerous plastic surgery interventions...

CF: *I'd like to invite you to contrast two authors who perhaps synthesize, through their lives, work and attitude, feminism and femininity: Simone de Beauvoir and Anaïs Nin. Simone de Beauvoir, the founder of contemporary feminism, in the book she published in 1949, The Second Sex, dives into an anthropo-sociologic and theoretic study of the complexity of feminist themes. She concludes: "Women don't surpass the pretext," they "take the world's inventory without trying to penetrate its meaning." Powerful affirmations from a powerful woman. On the other hand, Anais Nin is the quintessence of femininity. They were both not only authors, but were bestowed with a power of seduction over many artists and intellectuals who orbited in their sphere of influence.*

SM: As I read the biographies of Anaïs and Simone, in fact written by the same writer, Deirdre Bair, one of the things that instantly came to mind was the role which physical appearance plays in the way a woman sees the world, or formulates her theories about life in general. Nin has been described as an attractive woman, sensual, mysterious. When one watches films in which she was interviewed, the viewer is confronted with an elegance she exudes in everything she says and does: her elegant hands, her languorous gestures but in particular the timbre of her sing song voice, the cadence of her speech mirrored in her elegant writing with a profound belletristic character. Over her lifetime, Nin became a tireless master of the introspection of the inner emotional and erotic feminine landscape, explored in particular within her 78 journals written and published over a period of 60 years.

As for de Beauvoir, before diving into her biography, I listened to some of her dialogues on Youtube and was struck by a strident and somewhat brittle voice, by a person who does not give much attention to gestures or to her appearance in general. Simone is described as being intelligent and precocious from early on, while at the same time displaying clumsiness and gracelessness, a lack of interest in her looks, adamant in her urge to dominate her playing companions in their games, in taking over and leading their play; her father told her that her thinking was like a man's, and in the family's ether the concern for her chances to secure "a good match" was a persistent constant.

During her life, de Beauvoir established a feminist existentialism, which has fomented a moral revolution, giving credence to the claim that women are just as capable as men to choose and to reach a position of responsibility for their own self and in the world. She herself was a symbol and a model of feminism for her time. These two types of qualities which these two prominent women were endowed with may very well have influenced their theory about women's roles. And I wonder if, after all, they are not the very quintessence of these two notions: femininity and feminism?

Anaïs Nin slowly detaches herself from the feminist movement over her lifetime (an association which was in fact disputed by many from the start), while Simone de Beauvoir is considered, especially in the academic milieu, as the "mother of the post-1968 feminism."

I believe that these two women represent two powerful paths, original and very different, of exploring the status and the role of the woman.

Regarding Success, Happiness Simplifies Us.

CF: *One of our obsessive ideals in today's world—our competitive and energy devouring world—is achieving success. And yet another coveted ideal is happiness. Some even justify happiness through the achievement of success. For the majority, success means money, and achievement is translated in terms of financial accomplishments. How would you define happiness and how can "success" be achieved with the tools of spiritual psychology?*

SM: From the angle of spiritual psychology, happiness and success often mean something different than the tangible accomplishments promoted by mass media or that of today's cultures and civilizations. If we have to choose being loyal to our soul or loyal to certain morals, dogmas or societal expectations, we choose loyalty to our soul. That is where the secret of our happiness and success resides.

For example, a young man chooses a path that brings him less financial gratification in his career but is aware that it brings him more satisfaction than the path suggested by the "well intentioned" people in his life. Or, two people who love each other and find each other in different marriages where appearances are kept in the name of morality and ethics, decide to risk being together, sacrificing what is morally accepted in society because they understand that being together is part of their soul's evolution.

"Achieving success" in this life may also mean being conscious of our spiritual forefathers, who are not necessarily the founders of the religion we were born into, or one we adopt through marriage. The spiritual tribe we belong to is often discovered or rediscovered along our life's path. The signals appear during experiences which reveal the divine to us, during circumstances when we are abruptly overtaken by a sublime inner peace, or when we find ourselves in places where we are overcome by a deep awareness of belonging and of the eternal.

From the spiritual psychology perspective, being happy also means seeing that the glass is half full, being attentive to the big and the small occurrences, recognizing the miracle that exists in one's universe, from the entrancing beauty of a flower to the gift of our daily bread. Being at peace or "happy" may also mean inhabiting the awareness of abundance, and that of having or being "enough"... This is definitely more a state of mind and spirit rather than a certain amount in the bank, a list of properties or a certain social standing. I say this aware of the fact that in Los Angeles I am surrounded by friends and acquaintances who are millionaires many times over, whose walls are covered with diplomas and who are incredibly stressed about tomorrow, worried that even with all the effort and intensity they put forth in their work, they may not be able to maintain their material security and professional success for their entire working years, or that they won't be able to leave behind a legacy that would ensure their children a similar lifestyle.

I also know college scholarship recipients within our program—the Blue Heron Foundation Program— who for the first time were able to afford to move and pay rent for an apartment. They bought pillows and bed linens and a small refrigerator and felt that they'd "made it," that they achieved a standard of living that is not only sufficient but actually rather lofty, abundant. Having enough is often an imaginary horizon that keeps getting further and further away from us, hypnotizing us, entangling us in materialism's tentacles.

And last but equally important, I speak from my own experience. As an immigrant, I experienced all stages: of having comfort in my country of origin, of losing it all when we left, of starting to build from nothing, then having again...These experiences kept me from identifying success with the accumulation of material goods or my social standing. Our power is often limited when it comes to influencing bigger-than-life external forces molded by currents we cannot control. We always have, however, the ability to decide how to relate to these circumstances. Happiness, in this context, meant coming to terms with what is truly real, beyond the role of "success" in physical reality.

Being successful from a spiritual point of view also means that you yearn to heal yourself, to forgive others and yourself, that you are open to becoming increasingly aware of the humanity that exists inside of us, all of us. This inner process of forgiveness has to repeat continuously in order to evolve, in order to set foot on the next step of one's potential, of continuously transforming into your better version, aware of divinity and of one's sacred mission on Earth.

CF: *Still, people are haunted by failures, fears, depression; they often feel condemned to unhappiness. Earth is populated by souls adrift, much more so than souls at peace. Could a spiritual education help them?*

SM: The ability to extract that which we experience during meditation or prayer, during the transcendental moments of our lives, and integrate it into our daily experiences (at work, within our family, etc.), is a worthy spiritual exercise. I consider it much easier to attain by a monk or a nun who often live removed from worldly life, in environments that favor deep silence, introspection, a closer connection with nature, as opposed to the almost crazy whirlwind in which the majority of our lives unfold. However, I am an optimist, and I tend to think, to hope, that inner and outer spiritual forces will become our allies, so that a much larger proportion of the population will be guided to allow their existence to unfold toward a more evolved, more peaceful consciousness, closer to nature, closer to the light, less alienated.

CF: *Do you believe that the political and economic upheavals of today are somewhat related to the so-called spiritual decay of our world?*

SM: From my perspective, I see opposing forces that are profoundly influencing the political and economic climate of our times. On the one hand, we are becoming increasingly aware of the greed and self-ishness we've indulged in during the past centuries, especially starting with the industrial era to the present moment. This awareness is a good thing. In the States, there are an increasing number of books being published exploring the notion that our children's generation (the "Millennials") is the first generation who will have a lower standard of living than their parents', due to the excessive exploitation of natural resources, population growth, a globally inflated notion of what a comfortable life should be, as well as excessive consumption.

Comfort per se could be considered a vice, which could lead to a great deal of indifference in the larger social tableau, not unlike individualism which, along with its positive aspects, has led to a radicalization of competition, and has possibly been responsible in great part for the high levels of contemporary stress. As well, there are forces that are self-created, unwanted but inevitable, like the huge financial debts our nations face, funds allocated for wars (in 2009 alone, over 50% of the total money paid in taxes was used for military costs in the Iraq and Afghanistan wars, a total of over $1.5 trillion!), and the vulnerability of the worldwide banking system.

I remember hearing a statistic once that if every person in the world would have the standard of living of the average American, with the 2-3 cars per family, the 2000 gallons of water used daily, with all the food (especially meat) we consume, with all the laundry and dry cleaning, etc., we would need 26 planets Earth to accommodate these needs. And so, we are forced as a nation, but also as a planet, to change our expectations. And let's not forget that the commercials which transform every mortal into a consumer have penetrated to even the smallest and most modest villages on distant continents, where these advertisements seduce the aspirations of the local people toward the Western dream of a "comfortable life"... and who is to say that each person who could never afford more than a bicycle is not entitled to dream of owning a shiny car?

And so, to finally answer your question, I believe that we will be obligated to also look beyond the material satisfaction we draw from the tangible, physical world, and beyond indifference, selfishness, greed, corruption and violence, and start envisioning a world richer in experiences that deeply nourish our souls' aspirations.

Do We Still Read?
What and How Much?

CF: *At what age did you start reading and which book left a deep impression on you?*

SM: I am not sure it was truly my first book, but I remember *The Great Legends of the World*, which I read in third grade. I thought it was a great undertaking, a very thick book, but I braced myself and started with "Gilgamesh," the first story and the shortest one. I was fascinated and seduced by a world I had only intuited existed... To this day, the legends and myths of the world represent a fountain of inspiration to which I continuously return. Later on I discovered Joseph Campbell and the classic *The Power of Myth*.

CF: *And recently, what books have you read?*

SM: *Laughing Without an Accent* by Firoozeh Dumas, Benjamin Moser's *Why This World: A Biography of Clarice Lispector*, and *A Good Indian Wife* by Anne Cherian; I also reread two books that left an impression on me years ago: *Living History* by Katharine Graham and *Finding Your Element* by Ken Robinson.

CF: *Do you believe that a good book can carry you into a trance?*

SM: Yes, definitely. While reading adventure books (Alexandre Dumas, Karl May, Mark Twain) and love novels, (*Gone with the Wind* and *Jane Eyre*) during adolescence, the standard reactions from my parents were: "Why don't you grab the math book for a while and study? You get lost in those novels. How is that serving you?" or "Why don't you go outside, get some fresh air; it's been hours since you put that book down." And more than often my parents would return home from work at the end of a grueling day during my summer breaks and find me still in bed with the same pajama on, hair a whirlwind, hungry, holding on for dear life to the book I had started in the morning. Surely d'Artagnan's destiny was more urgent than the life I was living.

Even today, in my very busy and fairly demanding life, the thought that I could spend several days doing nothing but eating a little and reading for hours without being disturbed is a fantasy, a Utopia on the same level of others' dreams of luxurious vacations to exotic islands or high end destinations with elevated crowds.

CF: *During communism, reading was a serious occupation for the majority of the population. Lacking so many other things, devoid of liberty and opportunities, people took refuge in books. In every home, even the modest ones, there was a bookcase filled with books. Reading had not only a cultural role, but also a therapeutic one; it was a source of endurance during a dictatorship, a wellspring of survival and mobility in a society that was impervious and static. However, in this cliché tableau of the pre-revolutionary period, an essential element was missing: the joy of reading. But certain individuals were truly reading for pleasure. I believe that these very same individuals, even after the fall of the dictatorship and the acceleration of time, still read out of pleasure. Has your relationship with reading changed after you emigrated?*

SM: One of the reasons I was enamored with these books' worlds during adolescence was the fact that I could transport myself to eras and places I would have never accessed otherwise … and there was so much to learn and no other way of attaining that information. I was living in a confined Romania, where, because of communism and the lack of contact with the wider world, I felt that the books' role was essential in order to create rich and varied sources of reference, to understand more deeply who I was, to find role models.

Often, the immediate surroundings do not offer you the wisdom, the information or the role models one needs to fully develop. I considered it extremely important to immerse myself in how Balzac or Voltaire, for example, saw the world through their characters and to prepare for life with the help of minds more illuminated than those surrounding me. My thinking was that I would overcome difficult situations if I was armed with solutions already figured out by complex, mature characters overcoming extreme difficulties. Indeed, my relationship with reading changed during the decade following our emigration to the U.S.; this change was not for some frivolous reason but because I had no other choice.

Shortly after arriving in the States at the age of 15, besides attending high school, I was forced to work modest jobs in order to cover my every day expenses. My steady job after school helped me afford everything my parents could not give me, from my first car, gas and insurance to contact lenses and inexpensive clothing. But it also left me with almost no time to indulge in my dearest hobby: reading. I'd come home from work past 10 at night, feeling unable to burn the candle at both ends day after day. Because of these circumstances, Mircea Eliade's *The Forbidden Forest* took me six months to read. I remember during those years a constant low-grade feeling of starvation, a hunger I was unable to satiate in the rhythm I needed.

While receiving my masters in spiritual psychology, we were asked to read very many books that belong to the New Age genre. I remember how fortunate I thought that opportunity was. Around that time I started to develop an interest in esotericism and mysticism, and I started deepening my interest and knowledge in the fields of spirituality and philosophy and how they intertwine with human nature. More than that, it made me change the lens through which I filter classical and contemporary literature. Thus, years later when I started reading Tolstoy, I had a very different view of the characters who were struggling with themes of morality or God.

Now, in my forties, I divide my time between being a mother, a wife, founder of a nonprofit organization (which continues to grow and become more complex by the day) and the time I dedicate to the arts, including reading and writing. Reading has become one of those activities that are part of multi-tasking (who would have ever thought it possible?). I read while on the treadmill and I listen to audio books while driving in the car (I hear audiobook sales will soon surpass those of paperbacks). At times, I allow myself the luxury to read before going to bed. I feel that reading before bed directs the brain toward a rhythm and a state where it relaxes and is able to nourish itself. A good book is for the brain what a delicious meal imbued with minerals and nutrients is for body.

CF: *We come from a world where a book represented hard currency. Back then, good books were sold, more often than not, in the underground. They were often used* *to reward doctors in exchange for their medical services or, in various circumstances, as peculiar bribes, something unimaginable in the U.S. But even in today's Romania, things have changed drastically. Are we experiencing a cultural or an economic recession? What do you think is the value of reading in the society you live in?*

SM: The power of books and the value of reading in the world in which my life unfolds vary, I would say. In our home I am probably the only person who inhabits the continuum of "reading for pleasure." After "torturing" my husband with many questions about reading, he confessed that his brain is tired after reading hundreds of pages of legal and business documents, dense e-mails and online news on a daily basis. The scarce free time he has, he spends with our children or watching a little TV. We do have some friends who are serious readers, but the proportion is unimaginably smaller compared to what I was surrounded by growing up, and equally slim compared to how many people watch sports now.

CF: *You have two sons in school. What do they read?*

SM: At the ages of 15 and 17, they read strictly what is asked of them at school, which takes them about 3-4 hours a week and is comprised of many of the classics: *Romeo and Juliet, The Odyssey, The Catcher in the Rye.* They most certainly would never show up for school without having read what was required of them, but they also never use reading for simple relaxation; they prefer computers (or anything that has a screen!) and they look at me with great surprise if I suggest that they pick up a book and relax by reading: "Get with it mom, nobody reads for fun anymore…"

Behind the Bedroom Door

"There are two ways to reach me: by way of kisses or by way of the imagination. But there is a hierarchy: the kisses alone don't work."
—Anaïs Nin

CF: *Are subjects such as sex or eroticism incompatible with spirituality?*

SM: Not at all. Recently I asked a dear friend, someone who is a doctor and a writer and whose opinion I respect greatly, someone who has followed our published dialogue: "You, as a man, what other theme would you like to read about?"

"It would be interesting to read about eroticism."

Well then, let's do it. Even though I may be inspired by Mother Teresa, I am equally captivated by the Mata Haris who have a heart, by modern women embodying the geisha archetype, and all-in-all by what goes on behind the bedroom door slammed by a wife who is sick of her roles—from career woman, wife, mother, hostess—played to perfection outside the bedroom.

CF: *Eroticism, attraction and sex life change in a long-term relationship, especially after the kids arrive.*

What is there to be done to keep Eros busy with his seductive arrows?

SM: Besides the initial attraction—which, throughout the years, fluctuates—I believe that the principal factor that has to remain our priority is open communication. In a long-term relationship, our sex life becomes a byproduct of our verbal, emotional, spiritual and even subconscious communication. The more we are dedicated to the process of engaging in the river of life, as well as to that of personal transformation and the ability to express ourselves courageously, with honesty and from the heart, the greater the chances of experiencing a harmonious intimate life. And the more a couple has in common and the greater the ease of communication, the greater the chances of salvaging Eros.

And of course, we can't ignore the importance of consciously making an effort so that we move beyond stagnation. As cliché as it may sound, a caring note where we tell our partner what we appreciate in them, a present, a surprise, a trip (even something considered perverse by society—as long as we don't hurt ourselves or others), all these are ways of jolting routine and lifting that curtain that sometimes surreptitiously falls in front of our eyes, due to comfort, convenience, routine and a lack of vigilance.

CF: *How would you define sex?*

SM: First and foremost, sex is never just sex. It is an exchange of energy whose motivations vary from the infernal to the sublime. It is an expression of who we are and what we feel for the person we share that act with. It is a byproduct of that something that resides inside of us and cannot be expressed any other way: not in writing, spoken words, not through music or dance.

CF: *Is it important to maintain an emotional and erotic relationship outside the bedroom as well?*

SM: Yes, absolutely, because the bedroom is ultimately the last frontier. Again, we return to the multilevel communication that takes place outside the bedroom: the courage of honesty, that of perpetually finding paths to share, as well as the desire to rediscover our partner and remember what attracted us to him/her in the first place.

I should also add how important it is to maintain our devotion to our own self. Physically, we need to remember that our bodies are our souls' sacred temples and to care for their optimal, vibrant inner and outer health. Mentally, we have to remain engaged in the world, engaged in reading for example, to maintain our curiosity in subjects and areas that are of interest to us. Emotionally, we have to consciously remain dedicated to knowing ourselves, whether through the discipline of a journal or the journey of self-discovery and healing we can embark on with a therapist, where we learn to outgrow emotional patterns that no longer serve us. Spiritually, we nourish ourselves and grow through regular yoga, meditation, prayer, or contemplation with an intention behind it (it's important to always have a clear intention behind such practices).

I can't restrain myself from thinking a little more about the importance of intentions in our intimate lives. They can vary from "I will stay in this relationship until death do us part, no matter what" to "I will remain loyal to my soul in this relationship, and as such, I will always express that which unravels inside, AND IF our paths will not overlap anymore at some point, that is the signal that we are no longer meant to be together" to "we'll be together as long as I get what I want, or until my partner is what I want him/her to be." If we are unaware of our intentions, that which unfolds is still the product of our intentions, but subconscious ones.

CF: *In the world we live in today, the stressful, competitive world of today, eroticism as well as sexual relationships seem to be greatly affected, especially within the marriage. Where lack of sexual appetite is concerned, fatigue and worries are invoked as reasons, as well as a certain alienation that can occur within the relationship, at times originating either from the man's indifference or apprehension, or possibly, the woman's loss of feminine* *nature, or the loss of seductive appeal. Have sexual dys-funerions, impotence or frigidity on the one side and sexual dependency and immorality on another, compro-mised romanticism and eroticism?*

SM: I am sure that stories vary greatly depend-ing on the social circles we navigate. Every time I travel back to Romania, I seem to hear stories of women who give themselves too freely, and equally frequently, stories about unfaithful men; there seems to be an erotic energy there that is quite effervescent but also, in equal measure, a certain moral degrada-tion. Perhaps there is a higher way of channeling these sexual energies that goes beyond the polarities I wit-nessed there.

CF: *Based on your observations, could you synthe-size certain aspects, events connected to these extremes, as you call them, which perhaps can teach certain lessons that can be applied beyond the bedroom door?*

SM: I was talking earlier about inhibitions. A good friend of mine, American, beautiful and very sensual, confessed to me one day that in more than a dozen years of marriage she had not actually seen her husband fully naked ... not because he was not blessed by nature with a robust physique and a more than adequate phallus, but because he was extremely shy and wanted everything to happen with the lights off. After some years they divorced for other reasons. Her next lover was uninhibited and adventurous; he even "visits" her through the "back door" (to use her expression). But now she is the one who slips into judging herself that she may be doing something "dirty": "You see Stefania, these puritanical morals have been passed on to us and we've been brainwashed here in the States, sometimes in the most subtle ways, permeating and influencing our being. You were lucky to have been brought up in Romania..." The Snow White inside of me opened her eyes widely.

Or, if we talk about initiative and passivity, I also have friends who confess they feel proud of the fact that they play a passive role in the bedroom, allowing the men to unleash their passions uninhibitedly, assuming they are doing them a favor. Based on what I observe around me, I'd say that most people work arduously and when they arrive home in the evening, they are exhausted and prefer to play the passive role, hoping that the partner will be the initiator, hoping for seduction and a show complete with many highlights off of their favorite erotic menu ... not so much because they may be selfish, but because they are too tired. I remember someone once talking about taking turns, master and slave, and it hit me as being perceptive and democratic. For one, it dissolves the fear of accidentally playing the wrong role. And "the control" is divided somewhere in half (as the slave is the one in control).

One day, a Los Angeles friend of mine, a young mother, responded quite late to an email conversation that included several other Romanian-American ladies: "I'm sorry I didn't respond until now, I've been holding the baby in my arms for several hours and I can't write, he keeps pulling my hair and slapping me…my favorite thing in fact, but not from him!" In response, the other ones chirped quickly, "Mine too, mine too!" What is *this*? Even from respectable women? Could corporal punishment and hair pulling experienced in childhood, a common form of discipline in Romanian families back then, have started the programming of sadomasochistic behavior? In spiritual psychology it is said that the definition of healing is applying love on the wound that still hurts. Perhaps certain women are left with a yearning: to go again through that trauma, perfectly conscious that this time, behind the act of "punishment," there is nothing but love and a yearning to explore beyond the borders of what is common and bland.

Or, for example, one of my dear friends, on who nature bestowed a great deal of beauty, a beauty which in turn has been well preserved thanks to her aging genes but perhaps also due to her way of being (she doesn't seem to allow life's challenges to weigh on her too heavily), after fifteen years of marriage and two children, divorced. Two years later, she made the acquaintance of the brother of a close girlfriend, and it was obvious that the friendship she had embarked on was quickly transforming into love and that they wanted to honor that. Although he is decades younger, you cannot really see the difference in age; they are a harmonious couple in many ways. What amused me greatly was a comment she dropped offhandedly, something I didn't expect and which stayed with me because I thought it was a truth lived on a larger scale these days: "Well yes, I had to teach him how to make love properly; all those born after '85 behave in bed as if they were in porno films."

Her commentary resonates with various opinions about today's pornography. In the "olden" days, there seemed to be a curiosity with regards to exploring; you could sense the human being behind the "actor," there was somebody "home" in the eyes of the person. Now it is harder to decipher the soul in their eyes, and because of the explosion of the Internet, nothing normal incites anymore-—the "ordinary" seems boring. "We've seen everything and experienced nothing," remarked another one of my friends wisely.

CF: *And what is the connection between the divine act of lovemaking and spirituality?*

SM: It could possibly be the one my friend mentioned, at least for the women whose vaginas are connected to their hearts and their souls; specifically, all chakras, but especially the 2nd one, the one relating to creativity and sexuality, the 4th one, which is the chakra of the heart, and the 7th one, which is the crown chakra and represents our connection with the divine, have to be opened and aligned in order for us to experience that sublime act. It is possible that the orgasm is a micro experience of our union with eternity, a real life experience of a temporary death from which we are rebirthed … and for sure the quintessence of ecstasy. Impermanence, Eternity, Nirvana and Samsara … it's possible that all are concentrated in this one of a kind experience. It is important to understand where in the collage of our lives it has its place.

CF: *Could spirituality help the couple who is "adrift"?*

SM: Spiritually speaking, the more we are on the same wavelength with regards to our pursuits, communication, common values, even spiritual discipline (meditation, lectures, travels, etc.), the greater are the chances of the partners' hearts and souls vibrating on the same note, which ultimately can lead to a union on every level: physical, mental, emotional and spiritual. This, in my opinion, is a sublime union.

The Cycle of Existence

Let us learn to add life to our years, not just years to our lives.

CF: *In one of our previous discussions you were mentioning Samsara, a Sanskrit word, signifying the cycle of existence, essentializing the journey of the soul, the wheel of life continuously spinning between birth, death, rebirth. How and why did it reach your area of interest?*

SM: Samsara is a notion I thought about quite a bit during the past years. In part because it is the name of a movie produced by my husband, a film that took almost five years to make. Traveling with the crew to many of the locations in many countries, the fact that the film was edited and the soundtrack was composed in our home, that the director and the composer lived with us for about two years, made me contemplate this notion, and made me search for concrete examples or even metaphors which could lead to a deeper understanding of "Samsara."

I am a person who loves words, so to witness the expression of abstract notions such as Samsara in a non-verbal manner, only through images and music, was a one of a kind experience and one from which

I think I learned a lot. The film makers were pushed from the inside to explore ordinary man's search for the eternal and that which is timeless, and they gave their all so that the project could be polished to perfection with no pressure from film studios. Their intention was to bring to the audience an experience which, in spite of its inevitable impermanence, would stay in their hearts for a long time, make them contemplate what it means to live on this planet, all connected by common denominators that defy geographic borders, religions or races.

CF: *How would the abstract terms of "Samsara" and "Impermanence" be experienced in our daily lives and observations?*

SM: During these past five years I started paying attention to many cycles, micro and macro.

From the insects that are born, live a few days and die, to our nails' and hair's growth, nature's seasons, the holidays which repeat every twelve months, the birth, death and rebirth of passion inside ourselves and within a long term relationship, historical periods that last a few decades (say, communism), the cycle of an entire empire (Roman, Egyptian), the arc of a nation or race, or, for a moment, I can follow my imagination and contemplate the moment in time when the human soul was born, which, for the lovers of alternative history and esoteric information, supposedly took place 21.6 million years ago. Inevitably, the phantom of impermanence appears and with it questions bordering on obsession such as, "What is eternal?" "What doesn't change?" "Is it worth giving ourselves to the ephemeral?"

CF: *Well, is it?*

SM: Well, if we were to approach this matter realistically, for the majority of us, a hundred years from now nobody will utter our name anymore, nobody will know who we were; they certainly won't know anything about our achievements or failures, the loves or losses which marked us, the inner turmoil or restlessness which consume so much of our energy. This is seen through the realist's screen. But if we were to stretch a bit beyond the paradigm accepted by the majority of the population, we could contemplate something as esoteric as the notion of the Akashic Records, that "place" in the ether where our actions, emotions, words, thoughts, all our souls' experiences, are recorded for eternity. We are invited for a moment to consider a different paradigm. It is very possible that we'd take the same path on the physical axis whether we believe in the realistic or in the esoteric version, but the energy behind the actions may be very different if we believe that our deeds, thoughts, emotions, intentions and words are captured somewhere in the universe, for eternity. Perhaps we are then stimulated to relate differently to all that we do or think.

If we lose ourselves too deeply in the concept of impermanence, it is quite possible to fall prey to extremes. We can become adepts of nihilism. Or we can become very free and not let things get to us, moving fast in time and space, free of any commitments, because we can always tell ourselves: "What does it matter? Everything changes. Nothing stays the same."

And here is a more trivial example, one that I bump into every day and which I have studied carefully. Since I live in the "capital of the movie stars" where youth and the maintenance of the appearance are kept on a pedestal, I can't not think about physical deterioration, about getting old, about how we preserve ourselves, aware that time ruthlessly passes through everyone and that Impermanence, not Youth, is the true Queen of the Land. Every day we give in to our beauty rituals, today we get a blow dry and a manicure, tomorrow we go to the gym, afterwards it's the esthetician and the dermatologist's turn, etc., and in all this running around (and even when we feel for a fleeting moment that we sparkle and are put together from head to toe), we still have to maintain, without falling apart, the truth: that every moment we degrade one tiny bit and every moment we get a step closer to physical death.

So, what is worth investing time, attention, energy in if nothing lasts forever? This, too, presents an opportunity for less common answers. We can explore actions and give ourselves to noble aspirations that advance our individual dignity; or we can leave ourselves open to the moment, living it fully, accepting, savoring and suffering in the present. Can we do both simultaneously? Perhaps. To this, one could add the notion we continually struggle with, that of impermanence; thus we are juggling three axes, not an easy thing for the human psyche.

CF: *What other states does the term "Samsara" evoke in you?*

SM: Over time I've discovered countless feelings that I would categorize under Impermanence, nostalgia in particular among them (a character trait I've inherited from the paternal side of my family and which I've been wistfully rediscovering over and over at various crossroads), perhaps best exemplified by writings such as Proust's *In Search of Lost Time*. Not attaching ourselves to anything because of its transience is poignantly demonstrated in the film *Samsara* where the Buddhist monks in Ladakh, after days of creating an intricate mandala of rare beauty, destroy it as part of the ceremonial practice, an exercise in nonattachment.

CF: *You have, of course, been exposed to the birth of this film, participating in a cultural adventure that was* *extremely important and about which you continue to be passionate. Could you share a few highlights about the people you met or places you visited which left a mark on you?*

SM: One of the most memorable experiences during our travels was getting to know the members of the Himba tribe, a tribe belonging to one of the nomadic villages in northern Namibia, right at the border with Angola. Our family and the film crew were traveling together and we had to charter small, private planes for two separate trips in order to arrive at that faraway place, a place that felt like it inhabited the end of the earth. The airplane I was riding in had to circle several times, as the unpaved landing strip was covered with grazing goats, indifferent of our landing plans. In the village we met the members of the tribe, a tribe with a pastoral life that was both simple and primitive... a life that, I have to admit, seemed exceptionally beautiful, closely entwined with the rhythms and magic of nature, disconnected from materialism and all that which evokes "modern life."

I felt a sense of guilt when our younger son David, about nine years old back then, showed the tribe's chief his iPod as soon as he met him, transferring his headphones to the chief's head and pointing to the images of *School of Rock*. They had never seen a TV nor video images, nothing, and all of a sudden we had exposed him to the most commercial side of our lives. I had the sensation that we had introduced a virus...but had to come to terms with what had just happened and to accept that perhaps it would have been inevitable, even in the most isolated corners of the world.

The tribe's women seemed to be living a calm and harmonious life, mainly devoted to beauty and esthetics: their elaborate hairdos took daily adjustments; they were wearing rich jewelry made of natural materials, and skimpy but somehow stylish outfits that looked flattering on their long-boned, narrow bodies. Skin care was attended to several times a day through the application of an ointment (made of animal fat and ochre powder) which was meant to give them an even, reddish skin tone, as well as protect their skin from sun damage.

Their children seemed to have a deep sense of connection and community, physically were very well coordinated and were close to nature; they were helping one another, and I did not observe during my stay there much evidence of that sense of atrocious individualism or competition. Toward the evening, the men would return from hunting or from shepherding the goats. There was a lot of laughter; they seemed happy. I felt close to them, close to that whole scene.

CF: *Is it possible that many would see only the poverty, primitivism and the lack of hope of these disconnected-from-the-world tribes?*

SM: I notice a flutter of discomfort inside of me when I sense in those living in developed nations that they automatically pity these people, knowing very little about their experience beyond the obvious lack of Western goods. Among many such commentaries that collectively constitute this point of view, I remember one in particular that took place soon after Samsara came out. During a screening, in the middle of a scene where a Himba woman's gaze was piercing the audience with focused strength, the kind of look that is timeless and speaks directly to the soul, beyond historical, economical or cultural differences, the person behind me, all dressed up and adorned in matching jewels and makeup, exclaimed, "Ah, how sad!".

To me the look was dignified and magnanimous.

CF: *Still, your description gives us an idyllic and somewhat idealized image.*

SM: Of course there were great challenges as well. Malaria, an incurable disease, and skin cancer were the two main causes of mortality. Life expectancy was about fifty-two years of age, and the closest hospital, where the services offered and the equipment available were minimal, was many miles away. They also had to confront capricious weather and harsh winters, which forced them to migrate to milder climates and allowed no breaks from the unceasing effort to provide food and shelter.

One day we visited a tiny "school," a makeshift little encampment set up approximately seven miles away from the village. Our older son, Michael, who was eleven years old at the time, was touched by the scene and spoke to the students through our translator, asking for a list of needed materials, basic things they wanted (soccer balls and jerseys among them). The kids seemed intelligent and very open, very friendly. Not all the kids from the villages in the area were attending school; those who did had to walk all those miles. But the main problem they were facing was a double-edged sword: the majority of the students were male and many were leaving to attend middle school and high school in cities, leaving behind a diminished number of young men in the tribe. This gender imbalance led to some men taking several wives. Polygamy was thus a byproduct of choosing an education.

After many trips to many countries over the years, I've come to the conclusion that every culture has positives and negatives, pluses and minuses, at all levels, and I saw many of these aspects reflected in the lives of the children. In the more advanced countries—especially big cities—I notice how many children are confined to their small apartments, far away from nature's mystery, addicted to their screens, often overworked and not very emotionally present, less interested and maybe, due to circumstances, a little too free of the need to establish deep relations with their peers that transcend comparison and competition.

Perhaps the unhappiest children are the ones who have neither the advantages of the developed countries nor the connection with nature and the readily available love of family and community. I'm flooded with images filmed by the crew in the Philippines, where children were living next to a filthy, contaminated canal, where parents worked in harsh environments far away from home and conditions at school were below the minimal standards.

CF: *What was the impact of this world on your children?*

SM: I returned home with our two sons after a trip that lasted three weeks, while the crew followed its itinerary to other countries. School was starting five days later and we had to prepare. I remember this particular return because, for whatever reason, both kids were struggling with adjusting back to Los Angeles time. Finally, a day before school was to start, I decided to give each one of them half of a sleeping pill, in the hopes that they would sleep a few hours during the night. To this day, I am not sure it was the right decision, as they both became very agitated, and about half an hour afterwards, our oldest, Michael, burst into tears. I had a hard time soothing him, and I myself was shaken as he was behaving as if he had had a vision, some kind of abnormal and intense inner experience. I asked him "What's going on? What's happening with you?"

"Something's happened to me..." "What is it?" I insisted.

"I realized what life is all about."

I probably made some face, the result of being tired and somewhat worried that I wouldn't rise to the height of the moment. "I understand now that we live a very long life and that one day we all die," he explained. More sobbing. "And one day our dog, Kylie, will also be dead."

When our younger one, David, who was quite unsettled himself, heard this, he started crying out loud, "Kylie will die?!" They sobbed in concert and Michael continued: "And one day Kylie won't be here and none of my friends will be here either." The crying ascended to another octave, just as intense, the words were barely intelligible: "I know why we are here—to make something of ourselves. Every person on Earth is lucky. Don't waste time. I only have seventy years left to live. This is the message: don't waste your time; do something positive with your life." Then he added: "This is not our real life, the true one is beyond this experience."

After all the conversations about impermanence we had had during our trips, I felt at a loss for words at that moment. I had very much wanted to say something profound that would put a meaningful frame around that interior "a-ha" he had experienced, but all I was capable of doing that evening was to calm both of them down, lie next to them until they fell asleep and add one more episode to the notebook in which, over the years, I've chronicled some of their childhoods' highlights.

I felt drained at the end of that evening—physically, emotionally. When even the children join in with serious experiences and reflections about impermanence, reality in the present tense starts losing its footing and we get dizzy. They should be the very ones who help us plant our feet deep into the ground and allow us to temporarily forget about the passing of time, about physical death. That night, while trying to fall asleep, I remembered words I had read in a Buddhist book, a somewhat simple statement which had been haunting me because I could not make sense of it: "Samsara is Nirvana"... but now the meaning of it was starting to have contour: coming to terms with impermanence and accepting it *is* Nirvana, that place in the center of the wheel which is perpetually stable, the vantage point which sees the unfolding on the circumference of the wheel as something temporary and subject to the cycle of existence. To be conscious that there is a transcendental point from which we can see and accept the whole cycle... that is Nirvana.

For the moment I felt I had found the answer to the riddle and fell asleep.

What Dreams Tell Us

CF: *Have you ever kept a dream journal?*

SM: Over the years, I'd jot down the more vivid dreams in my regular journal, next to events, observations, reflections. As of 2011, I started keeping a journal solely dedicated to "direct knowing," i.e. intuitions, synchronistic moments and repeatedly occurring or vivid dreams. Although initially it was a requirement of the "Consciousness, Health and Healing" program I was attending at University of Santa Monica, I've continued to maintain a dream journal long after graduating from the program.

Even though I've always been a person conscious of being able to remember many of my dreams (it is said that we all dream between three and seven dreams every night), the fact that I was required to write them down daily, forced me to learn certain techniques to maximize my ability to recall them. Firstly, before going to bed, I had to set an intention to remember my dreams; then, keeping a pen and paper next to the bed was crucial, as I could quickly jot down a few words in the middle of the night or early morning, so that during the day I could record the entire dream. Another method is to not speak or leave the bed in the morning before writing down the gist of the dream. A technique I have often used during the mornings when I could absolutely not remember the dream, was to come back to the physical position I was in when I first woke up and go down the list of the most important people in my life; it is said that the majority of the dreams we have are about the same eight or ten most important people in our lives.

CF: *What can we learn from our dreams? Are they capable of explaining our past, shedding light on the present or anticipating future events?*

SM: Jeremy Taylor, one of the most respected writers on the subject, added to the title of his book *The Wisdom of Your Dreams* the subtitle *Using Your Dreams to Tap into Your Unconscious and Transform Your Life,* a subtitle which I consider an answer to the question "Do dreams serve us?" In my opinion, dreams offer us a path of understanding, at times of anticipating or preventing something, of deciphering mental and emotional patterns, a way to heal or appreciate beauty and harmony in a profound way, a place where our day-to-day consciousness cannot reach given its limitations.

For those who have formal studies in psychology or psychiatry, and even for "the rest" of us (in the end, we all have a certain expertise in the human condition, regardless of our educational background), there is an awareness that there are contradictory aspects within us. There are aspects we try to understand and integrate, so that there is an inner—albeit temporary—harmony. I consider dreams an essential part of our mental/emotional/spiritual life which, with careful observation and thoughtful interpretation, help us, in perhaps a discreet but essential way, to reach an important inner balance. The journey of becoming acquainted with our dreams is really the journey of becoming acquainted with our unconscious; it represents not only the sought after opportunity of healing the wounds that sabotage our lives, but an attuning to guidance that is profoundly uplifting and freeing.

Dreams are perhaps the oldest archetype we can access, the oldest treasure left by our forefathers, before language took being, before hieroglyphs or cave paintings came into existence; they are the leitmotifs connecting us to our ancestors from hundreds of thousands of years ago, the bridge connecting us with so-called "alternative history." In our dreams we visit that "collective unconscious," the dream bank where tens of thousands of generations of our human species deposited the wealth of the journeys that took place once they drifted to sleep.

CF: *Are there many types of dreams? What should we consider when categorizing them?*

SM: I know that experts have their firm beliefs. Of course, I only speak from my experience (which has, however, been purposefully and diligently cultivated over the years), as well as from numerous materials I read on the subject. As such, I found that there are many different types of dreams, but three main categories stand out for me. Astral dreams are the dreams where the spirit of the person asleep travels through galaxies, or visits our Terra of millions of years ago where the continents had a different configuration, or is even projected ahead in time. The second group of dreams is where we process what has happened the previous day or week, bits and pieces of conversations, incidences or people who were part of what unfolded during that time. The subconscious is most likely attempting to process and discharge excess material that clutters our inner pathways.

The third category is perhaps the one Freud was referring to when he declared that dreams were the "royal road to the unconscious," and here I would list the dreams where a plethora of incidents take place and where the subconscious, that " basement" that is dark during the day, becomes filled with light and no detail remains in the shadow. By analyzing that type of dream, we can become aware of what is truly happening in our conscious life, where the curtain which helps us repress the hurtful reality of certain truths or incidents, is suddenly lifted.

I should also mention prophetic dreams (especially the foreboding ones) as well as lucid dreaming (when we are aware that we dream and decide to play a conscious role in our dream) and repetitive dreams (where we try to resolve a pattern essential to our current consciousness), which will be repeated until the wound is healed or overcome. In these dreams we discover projections and self-deceptions which, far too often, interfere with honest, warm and authentic communication between parents, children, lovers, friends, colleagues, authorities, temporary acquaintances etc. This is also the realm where an artist, a scientist, an inventor etc., finds a solution to a problem he has assiduously labored over during the day. The experiences in which Einstein, Mendeleev or Bohr have finally found the answer to a long belabored research question in their dreams are well documented. There, the walls of the conscious mind and imagination collapse, giving the individual the opportunity to achieve a breakthrough.

There is such a notion as "dream incubation," where indeed, the idea is to ask ourselves a question before going to sleep, with the intention of gaining clarity with regards to a challenge we face. Often, the solution appears in a dream and at first sight may seem unrelated to the issue, but, upon deeper analysis of the dream (often through the "Gestalt" method where we give a voice to every character/animal/object present in the dream), we start deciphering deeper themes, which are often connected to the challenge we want to overcome or understand in our conscious reality.

CF: *What is the power of prophetic dreams?*

SM: I do believe in these type of dreams, although I only rarely have them. Here is an example from my own journal: on December 26th, 2011 I dreamt that I met one of the seminal inventors of the 20th century, who had died two months prior. In the background, there were the stars of our galaxy, although it seemed we were sitting in a universe outside of time and space, at least the way we perceive time and space on Earth. He seemed in rather good spirits and expressed his delight over having transitioned to another dimension. He communicated (in that telepathic way in which we communicate in our dreams), that he was feeling much freer in that dimension, that he could travel faster, help more, that he was feeling less inhibited. I was rather touched by his jovial, happy-go-lucky disposition. When I woke up, I wrote down the dream and shared it with my husband.

Three days later, our foundation's vice-president called to tell me that a couple of days earlier, an American of Romanian origin who worked for that inventor's company had pledged a $10,000 donation to our foundation which was going to be doubled by the company's matching gift program. Honestly, it was for the first time that I became conscious of a dream that would so clearly show a prophetic connection between the reality of our physical world and the world "behind the curtain," our dream world. I knew clearly that had

I not remembered the dream and written it down, the whole synchronicity would have eluded me, the way the majority of connections between the dream world and the physical world elude us. I realized that in the dream, the notion of time is different, that we can travel in the past and the future without obstacles, and, even more, I became profoundly conscious that tracking dreams is a discipline which helps us connect more directly with the world of the unseen, that ether which, while consciously awake, we only intuit.

Another prophetic dream took place during the night of December 27th, which, in the Romanian Orthodox calendar, is the night of Saint Steven. So on that night I dreamt of an old college friend of mine whose name was Stephen. I met him during my undergraduate days at the University of Utah, and he had invited me to visit Los Angeles on a couple of occasions. We had kept in touch over the years and celebrated each other's accomplishments. Stephen was a handsome man with a big heart who eventually became a caring doctor, yet in his early 40's he still hadn't found the love of his life. I had made mental notes about the qualities he was hoping for in a woman, and kept my radar ON for such an appearance.

All this information is useful as a background for the dream I had: I was spending an evening with Stephen, as friends, enjoying each other's company the way good friends do. In the dream I was playing the role of some kind of a leader, exposing him to unexpected positive experiences; suddenly, our walking evolves into flight and we were flying above the roofs of the houses. Flying happily, stopping every once in a while and looking through a window into people's homes, afterwards continuing our flight. I was wearing a yellow chiffon dress; the rest of the characters and the background were all dark colors. The feeling I had in the dream was that I was easing the pathway to the experience of JOY, a state he had forgotten.

The next morning, a girlfriend, who months ago I had asked to write down the qualities of her ideal partner (an old habit of mine), confessed to me she was ready for a long-term relationship: "so, if you know of anyone…" The fact that I had dreamt about Stephen and had written down the dream immediately afterward brought him to the forefront of my mind, along with the qualities he had described as desirable in a woman. I told my girlfriend that I only knew one person I thought would match her description, and I put them in touch. What followed, according to them, was many get-togethers that mirrored the elated exuberance in my dream. I interpreted the dream as an augur for a state which he hadn't felt in a long time, and my role as a guide to reaching that state by introducing them to each other.

CF: *After this story, you may find yourself assaulted by people who have written their ideal scene for an intimate relationship, hoping you can somehow make it come true.*

SM: I can't hold back a smile. It seems that things unfold in such a way that I'm only asked to do what I can, for whoever I can, at the opportune moment. I've discovered a certain elegance in the way the universe arranges things.

CF: *Can we make our subconscious an ally in our dreams and can we "coach" it to serve us?*

SM: The Tibetan Buddhists and the shamans have a tradition of working with their dreams, an approach that is supposed to be more than a thousand years old among Buddhists and many thousands of years old among shamans. In Buddhists' spiritual lives, dreams have a profound importance on several levels: starting with their roles of predicting (auspicious dreams of the mothers of the Dalai Lamas before their births), warning (the dreams of monks in which ominous signs that the Dalai Lama's life is in danger occur) to viewing life as "empty, without substance, like a dream," and the belief that when a person dies, he enters a dream from which he never wakes up. By contrast, shamans use dreams to gain perspective and fascinating insights, from healing (where a shaman can enter directly in the dream of the person who is in need of healing and perform a ritual) all the way to integrating an individual's vital energy with the archetypes of the broader life of the cosmos.

Vital Energies

"We are coming to understand health not as the absence of
disease, but rather as the process by which individuals
maintain their sense of coherence (i.e. sense that life is
comprehensible, manageable, and meaningful) and the
ability to function in the face of changes in themselves
and their relationships with their environment."
—Aaron Antonovsky

CF: *Life's ever turning wheel is not just an existential unfolding, but an energetic one as well, and the chakras—a word of Sanskrit origin which may very well be translated as "wheel"—are defined as subtle concentrations of energies which, it is said, maintain our physical and spiritual equilibrium. Have you ever been tempted to explore this subject?*

SM: I have read about the chakras for a while now, but have not tried to have a direct experience until 2008, when I spent a whole year trying to work with these energies very directly. I used to wake up early in the morning and dedicate almost every day of the week, a whole hour from 5:30 to 6:30, to seven guided meditations that focused on each chakra. There were a few elements which proved to be very helpful in being especially attuned to these experiences: my lifelong propensity to be a dedicated autodidact; the deep desire to accumulate notions from many areas; my continuous intention of applying and experimenting with everyday life "theories" I had read about; the experience I had when I trained for two whole years as a competitive gymnast at Onești, "the" Romanian gymnastics school, during the years when Nadia Comaneci was there; and finally, the ambition to keep my physical health through yoga and ongoing physical exercise. Through these last two experiences in particular I learned that the mind-body-soul connection is of the utmost importance.

CF: *Tell me more about the Onești period. Did you train as a competitive gymnast?*

SM: I trained competitively but did not make it beyond modest national competitions. What stayed with me was the discipline of working out every day, persevering in the mind-body connection and experiencing the joy of feeling strong, fit, and able to do a great many things with my physical body. That is pure joy, and I kept that throughout the years, to this day. Beyond that, while at Onești, I had experiences that may seem sad to most people, but viewed through another filter, they may be considered absolutely perfect learning opportunities for what ended up unfolding later in life. Living far away from home at such a tender age—3rd and 4th grade—I experienced the deep pain of feeling abandoned by my family and I identified deeply with abandoned children (mind you, the decision to attend was ultimately mine). Working through those feelings of deep suffering was a long term process, yet I remember I overcame the most biting part of it by the end of my first trimester there. As I started to relax more into my new environment, I began to discover the deep camaraderie that can blossom in dorms among students who live in boarding schools. With time, I ended up enlarging my horizons in ways I would have never expected when I first started school there: I landed the lead role in a play which was a big success in our dorms; I developed an enviable correspondence with countless relatives and friends, an activity that was a continuous source of emotional and spiritual upliftment; last, but certainly not least, I became an occasional "advisor" to the older girls in the matter of boyfriends! Half-jokingly, half seriously, they often solicited my advice: sometimes wise, other times unconventional, but always very different than what they were used to hearing, given that most girls came from modest villages around Onești while I was one of the few students who had grown up in Brasov, a vibrant city with cultural traditions spanning centuries. They named me "Little Miss Ambassador" and it stuck.

I also had some unusual experiences cast on the austere and unvaried backdrop of the communist landscape: Queen Fabiola of Belgium came to visit our school one day. I remember the afternoon when I had returned from the cafeteria only to find our dorms thoroughly transformed: colorful Persian carpets everywhere, flower arrangements placed artfully on tables and armoires, new paintings hanging on the wall! These objects had hurriedly been brought from the mayor's office and other state institutions in an effort to create an inflated impression about the luxury the Romanian government was lavishing on its champions and champions-to-be. The next day, of course, the ascetic backdrop returned. I was there during the period when American film crews were flooding our school (right after the '76 Montreal Olympics), collecting footage for TV documentaries about Nadia and the Olympic gymnasts. While those superb gymnasts were training for international competitions, Bela and Marta Karolyi were grilling them with their Svengali-like torrents of powerful energy, a mix of fear and character building. In spite of my mediocre progress in gymnastics, I was thrilled: I felt I was living in the place where the most captivating action—in the otherwise dormant, beige and grey country—was unfolding.

CF: *What is the role of the chakras and what is their relationship to spiritual psychology?*

SM: What I want to share with the reader is not so much relating to notions or theories pertaining to the chakras (because individuals who are much more knowledgeable are in a position to speak on this), but my experience as a lay person who put some effort into understanding and experimenting with them, and how all of this relates to our daily life in a very pragmatic way.

In simple terms, the chakras belong to an ancient spiritual system and are considered the sacred centers which transport us on our path to a deeper awareness, enlightenment and integration. Although some adepts work with a system of 12 chakras, others use a system of 7 or 8: 7 in the body and the 8th approximately 2 feet above the head, aligned with the main vertical meridians in the body.

CF: *Could you define these chakras and their roles?*

SM: Chakra #1, situated at the base of the spine, symbolized by the earth, exudes an energy red in color and it connects us with our physical body, the physical/tangible world; it is connected not only to issues of survival, but also to that "programming" done by our tribe and/or culture into which we are born.

Those whose 1st chakra is underactive, usually struggle with physical issues, struggle with survival or the feeling of belonging in the world they live in. For those who have an overly active first chakra, they are very materialistic, even greedy; they overidentify with their physical appearance (their body, clothing, the image they project etc.) or cannot see beyond the prejudices and misidentifications of the culture/tribe they were born in.

Ideally, if the person is well balanced in this first chakra, he/she would be a very grounded person, anchored in reality and physically healthy. This person is able to survive based on their own efforts and with the feeling that they have enough and there is enough; they enjoy prosperity and security.

CF: *For example, what is the state of your first chakra?*

SM: I have to confess it is an area where I had to invest a great deal of effort. Through self-reflection I came to realize that parts of my first chakra were underactive while others were overly active. First, all immigrants are vulnerable to imbalances in this chakra as the uprooting process affects it directly and they may be out of balance. Although I've never looked into scientific data, I hear frequently, in communities of immigrants past a certain age, complaints about health problems that correspond to this chakra, such as colorectal cancer and problems with the lower digestive tract.

CF: *And how could one prevent the diseases caused by this chakra?*

SM: The enticing thing about the meditation and balancing exercises is that we can work directly with our breath and visualization, the most frequent exercises being the ones where we visualize opening and closing a red color, four petal lotus; as well, specific exercises where we forgive ourselves for judging ourselves as guilty for a myriad of actions, thoughts or even fantasies. In addition, there are exercises for gratitude, gratitude for what we are, who we have become or were able to accomplish, and ultimately even inner commitments or notes written down in our journals, intentions for behavioral change. While practicing kundalini yoga throughout the years, I have also become familiar with specific physical exercises, sets known as kriyas which have been proven to target specific chakras, including the first chakra.

One of the elements I was happy to incorporate during these exercises was the deeper understanding of how I was "programmed" by Romanian culture, the religion I was born into, the communist system where I spent my childhood and adolescence, and the family values that were passed on. I could then decide, in a conscious manner, what I wanted to hold on to and what no longer served me and thus needed to be "pruned." It was important to me to complete, as consciously as possible, the inner collage of who I was: a global citizen of Romanian origin who chose to live a conscious life in the United States. Additionally, I integrated elements that bridge the relationship between the inner self and the physical world, especially when the outside world seems particularly harsh: deep breathing exercises and inner affirmations, along with a strong intention of maintaining my inner equilibrium, no matter what. This may seem rather simplistic, yet it has served me well throughout the years.

CF: *If the condition of knowing oneself better involves dedicated meditation, visualization exercises and journal writing, one may say, considering the accelerated world we live in—not only competitive, but devouring of energies—that it is a true luxury to set aside this kind of time, a luxury not many would be able to afford. Your example, however, could be a stimulus to many to "steal" time in order to balance and optimize their existence.*

SM: I am not sure that the secret lies in "stealing" time, but I've learned it is very important that at the end of the day we take an inventory and come to terms with what we invested our energy into and what we received in return. Let's just suppose that at the beginning of each day we all have 100 units of energy, and in the evening, when we tally up, we realize we invested 30 units in a relative who gave nothing in return. Now we are left with 70 units (if indeed all other investments went well and gave us a similar number of units in return). A question that bears asking thus is: what people, projects or inner patterns contribute to our energy, elevate us, and which ones devour our energies on a regular basis ... and what are we willing to change? The idea here is to become aware of the subtlest energetic investments, of clarifying our priorities and ultimately aiming to not be in the red day after day, month after month.

It is because we live in a world where the majority of us have a very full schedule, are stressed and stretched at the seams even in our limited free time, that I insist on the idea of knowing ourselves and respecting our priorities. I, for one, have arranged them in a hierarchy which organizes and clarifies my life and which brings me inner peace when I respect it: 1) my relationship with the divine 2) my relationship with myself 3) my relationship with my immediate family (husband and children) 4) the foundation I run and my extended family and 5) social relations, hobbies, etc. I have become deeply aware what activities/people/inner preoccupations fill me to the brim and I'm grateful I've learned to say "no," with no trace of guilt, more and more often to activities or invitations which are not aligned with my inner priorities.

CF: *Can you elaborate on the association between chakras and colors that you mentioned before?*

SM: Sure. For example, chakra #2, represented by the element of water, situated in the area of the genital organs, corresponding to the development stage of 6 to 24 months, emanates an orange color and is the quintessence of creativity, feeling, emotions and all that relates to our sex life. This chakra is responsible for closing contracts between two people, whether it is a business contract, an emotional one or one of a sexual nature. When this chakra is in equilibrium, the experience we have is one of grace, fluidity and openness toward people. We have the strength to live powerful experiences (without constantly complaining) and to generate sexual experiences which are deeply satisfying and do not contradict our values; we have the ability to express ourselves creatively, with grace and ease, without inhibitions or obstructions.

CF: *Can you illustrate this chakra through a situation you experienced?*

SM: About five years ago I had an interesting experience that exemplifies what it means to be aware of this chakra's energy. I was introduced to a man about 50 years old, someone I was told was a powerful businessman.

We shook hands and right away I felt as if someone had punched me in the lower abdomen (in the area corresponding to the 2nd chakra); I also sensed right away that I could see a very muddy grey around this person. Later on, I found out from some mutual friends that his intimate life was based on paying "professionals" and that his proclivities revolved around "roughness" in the bedroom, which he was inflicting on others but not open to receiving himself.

What also comes to mind is how a nation relates to the 2nd chakra. From experience and observations, I would say that overall, in the United States, a great deal of the population is still heavily influenced by puritanism, and the confines of what is permitted are fairly narrow. A lot more often than in Romania, for example, an affair leads to divorce, or the appearance of a mother not wearing a bra at a school event causes whispers of opprobrium. For sure American feminists would start a revolution if they would receive even one of the Romanian chain emails I sometimes get on the subject of women. This is from only the week before: Five thieves caught a nun in the forest and raped her. She walked away crossing herself: "Thank you God; satiated *and* sinless."

CF: *I like to think that humor is good for all chakras.*

SM: Political correctness is sometimes humorless.

CF: *But sometimes the Anglo-Saxon austerity is preferable to mockery and triviality.*

SM: There is something to be said about stimuli that keep our mind sane and our body healthy. Chakra #3, represented by the fire element, situated right where the solra plexus is, corresponds to the stage of development that unfolds from 18 to 36 months. It emanates a yellow energy and it is the center of our personal power, our autonomy and independence. It is the chakra responsible for courage and our metabolism.

When it is well balanced, it provides the energy for initiative, efficiency, spontaneity and a kind of power that doesn't aim to control or conquer. It is the chakra of our ego, the part in ourselves where we are conscious of who we are as individuals. It is also the place where we compare ourselves, often unconsciously, against standards and ideals accumulated throughout our lifetime, at times adopted consciously, but often unconsciously, by our inner mechanism. It is the chakra on which I have spent the most amount of time. I think almost half of all my work on chakras over the years was dedicated to this particular one... The trilogy of the first three chakras is definitely the one that monopolizes most of our attention, at least for most of us mere mortals.

CF: *I understand that chakras can influence our sense of wellness and state of equilibrium. How do we know if one or more chakras are out of balance? And what do we do then?*

SM: We are often made aware of which chakra is out of balance by actual physical symptoms. In my case, for example, throughout the years, I've always had to pay attention to my adrenal glands, which correspond to the 3rd chakra and for which I've had to take certain natural drops that strengthens them, in order to maintain their optimal functioning. Throughout my life, I had experiences where I'd get up in the morning, conscious that there was a ball of apprehension and fear in my stomach, the worry of overlapping with the trials and tests of the physical world vividly felt. For sure, this sensation was a sign that this chakra was out of balance. In this case, a meditation where I was visualizing a yellow ten petal lotus slowly opening (with each expiration) and closing (with each inspiration) in the region of my solar plexus has been of great help. In addition, I repeated an inner affirmation related to personal self-empowerment (the power that doesn't seek to dominate or control), meant to strengthen my inner faith. This inner trust I consider important to spring from a deep place within ourselves, the place where we contend with life and prove to ourselves that we are capable of winning at least some of the battles, the place where we prove to ourselves that we have the courage to go on.

CF: *I like the fact that you try to find everyday parallels so that the notion of chakras is more easily understood. Thus, the imbalance of the first chakra, if I understood correctly, could be translated as "having your head in the clouds" and that of the over activation of the third chakra could be understood as "having butterflies in your stomach." Could you explain the fourth chakra in a way we can all understand?*

SM: Given the fact that the whole notion of chakras could seem rather exotic, I tried indeed to find examples in popular idioms. That way one realizes not only that they can be easily understood, but that we Westerners, too, are more familiar with them than we imagine. They've always existed, whether we called them chakras or something else. I've tried to find examples in English idioms, literature and music in order to dissipate the intimidation the reader may feel. Thus, in those moments in our lives when there is an imbalance in our fourth chakra, we may recognize it when we hear something like "she broke his heart," "And in my heart there stirs a quiet pain" (Edna St. Vincent Millay, "What lips my lips have kissed, and where, and why," Sonnet XLIII), "I shook his hand, and tore my heart in sunder,/And went with half my life about my ways." (A. E. Houseman, "He would not stay for me, and who can wonder"). The healing and rebalancing of this chakra may be described as, "a load off my chest," "a sigh of relief" or "Christ, strengthen my heart."

Thus the fourth chakra is the chakra of the heart. It emanates the color green and it is the center of love, compassion, the ability to accept ourselves and others, the ability to forgive as well as to hope; it is the energetic center for inner peace, and, many would say, the strength of putting, when needed, the reins of Destiny in God's hands.

CF: *What would be signs of its dysfunction?*

SM: The "malfunctions" would be expressed through jealousy, possessiveness and dependency.

One may have "a heart of stone" or may be unable to establish stable, strong and authentic relationships.

The characteristics of these individuals may often be timidity, loneliness, isolation, bitterness and an excessively critical attitude.

CF: *Have you had experiences where your fourth chakra was perturbed? If so, how did you heal?*

SM: Because my studies and experience are in applied spiritual psychology, I've always been stubborn about putting into application the theoretical notions I learn. Yes, to be alive means to experience such impasses. It happened some years ago, with a person who, whenever I was around her, made my heart feel heavy. I knew things were not ok between us. We had dissected our differences endlessly but could not reach an understanding, and it became clear that the distance that had been created between us could not be resolved through endless conversations or analytical dialogues. And because it had also become clear that neither one of us would leave the relationship, and because I knew myself enough to know I could not sustain such an unhealthy mode of relating, I decided to put myself through the following process: every day for forty days I sat down in silence and visualized a bridge of light connecting our hearts.

The truth is that I had no clue, on the conscious level, how the misunderstandings would resolve themselves. But my intention and visualization were strong and clear: to open our hearts and to melt the layer of unforgiveness that had been created. In these times of great speed and superficiality (especially in Los Angeles, my adoptive city), these types of approaches may seem incredibly "costly," but as far as I was concerned, the final result was worth the investment many fold. In Romania we have an expression "love understands all languages;" in other words, it is the only universal language...a very lovely way of saying that love exemplifies the approach described above—a process of the heart that goes beyond language or words.

CF: *What color is the fifth chakra?*

SM: Situated in the region of the base of the neck, it is the energetic center which emanates the color blue and is responsible for everything that relates to communication: from the intonation of the voice, to how well we are able to listen to someone, our ability to express ourselves clearly and concisely, the ability to honor and communicate our inner truth, of being determined and resolute in making decisions. It also relates to non-verbal communication, including our e-mails or what we post on Facebook.

CF: *Would it be correct to say that if this chakra is out of balance the person is taciturn or excessively verbose?*

SM: The excesses may manifest themselves through gossip, a dominating voice, exaggerations; deficiencies would show up as excessive introversion, confusion, an exaggerated withholding or telling lies. Idioms that would describe these imbalances would be "spill the beans," "like talking to a brick wall" and "half the truth is often a whole lie," etc.

The most relevant experience I had with this chakra was during the brief period I pursued acting. Over the years, I have not only taken accent reduction classes to diminish my Romanian accent (rule of thumb is that all those who arrive in a new country after the age of 14 will have an accent) but also voice lessons, which focused on the ability to polish the timbre, the ability to connect to emotions and to project sound to the last rows of the audience (without screaming). My initially rather timid and high pitched voice became a stronger, more robust voice which I could also modify, depending on the character I was playing.

Another important aspect for me, and I sense for many others as well, is the desire to honor the truth through communication, regardless if it is uncomfortable, impolite or painful sometimes. It has perhaps been the hardest lesson for me, as I was brought up with values like "be respectful no matter what," "don't offend no matter what" and "don't hurt no matter what." But the price of adhering too tightly to those values proved to be too big. It took me years to understand the difference between being polite and sacrificing important information which had to be communicated lest the inner peace be disturbed forever, draining our vitality and diminishing our self-respect.

CF: *Is there a magic formula for keeping our chakras clean, in balance, efficient?*

SM: It is important to understand that it is almost impossible to keep all chakras working perfectly at all times. Understanding each chakra more deeply and attempting to balance them in a conscious manner helps us live a much more efficient life, energetically speaking, which ultimately means a life with more fullness and equilibrium. In order to strengthen a chakra whose energy has deteriorated, a long term investment of persistent discipline is sometimes needed. And, not to be redundant, but the process of forgiveness and self-forgiveness is of paramount importance in this process of healing out-of-balance chakras.

Perhaps in the beginning it may seem strange, but the exercise of placing one's hand on the heart and saying "I forgive myself for judging myself as not being wise enough, too weak, incompetent, untalented," etc., repeated many times, is a method of forgiveness which helps us graduate to the next level of self-liberation. Nothing weighs us down more than the heavy load of self-judgment which we gradually pile on, starting in our early childhood. And one of the next steps which aids this process of healing, is of demonstrating our gratitude for all that is good and positive that already exists in our lives: people, things, situations for which we feel truly blessed. Acknowledging that, for example, we have gratitude for our health, the roof over our head, a friend, the poems we read the day before or the upliftment we felt in our relationship with our spouse the other day, are as ordinary (and seemingly naive) as they are effective.

Had I not put into practice these exercises year after year, at least weekly if not daily at times, I would have never come to understand their profound effect on us and would have dismissed them as "pop psychology" exercises; done in a quiet place, with an authentic intention, they can bring deep purification, which, along with prayers (for those who pray) or meditation (for those who meditate), help maintain a clean interior that is less weighed down by misidentifications or futile patterns.

CF: *Is there a hierarchy in the importance of the chakras?*

SM: The higher we lift ourselves, and that includes the order of the chakras, the closer we get to divinity. The sixth chakra is the chakra of the third eye and it has a three-dimensional position: situated at the level of the midpoint between the eyes but deep inside, intersecting the path of the two optical nerves. It is the chakra that represents clarity and that helps us filter reality through the lens of wisdom.

Those whose sixth chakra is in balance tend to have a sharp memory and great intellectual capacities, are intuitive, have an elevated emotional intelligence, are capable of abstract, symbolic thinking and creative acts, and of accessing and interpreting dream symbolism; they have the strength for self-evaluation, the desire to see the truth, the ability to visualize, the quality of learning from experiences, of detaching and acting wisely. Those whose sixth chakra is deficient tend to live with suspicion and mistrust about their own self, and sometimes lag behind in sensibility; they repress their memories and their ability to visualize or to see a future is atrophied. They are scared of self-analysis, are rigid and tend to manifest hostility and jealousy, as they are in a constant process of comparing themselves to others. The "demon" of this chakra, if it can be called that, is illusion.

Perhaps we've all noticed this concentration of the third eye when studying Jesus's face on a fresco, a statue of Buddha, or the picture of a Hindu meditating in the lotus position. Even the rest of us, whether we meditate in the correct position, with the correct body alignment, or on our knees, immersed in prayer, can easily become conscious that energy is concentrated at that point exactly in the region of the third eye.

CF: *How can we let go of the "demon" of illusion?*

SM: Practically speaking, here are two examples of the way I worked with this chakra in an effort to discern illusion from truth. In the first situation, I was comparing myself to a friend who I thought had been blessed by nature with very many qualities. Many more than I had been. I was witnessing her earning her existence at a high level, being able to express her creativity, and being recognized for these qualities; at the same time she was physically attractive, efficient and courageous in business, warm and feminine.

I'd have to confess that this comparison could have only originated from my ego and belonged to this very chakra. Making something into a situation where you compare yourself to another and ultimately "win" or "lose" belongs to a dualistic model, as the conclusion easily shows: one has to be superior and one inferior.

If we were to filter this situation through the wisdom and compassion of the sixth chakra, surpassing illusion, then we'd come to the conclusion that every individual is unique, with his/her own destiny, each one with his/her beauty and richness, and cannot be seen or understood if we use a black-and-white or hierarchical lens.

Another example has to do with the romance experienced within the relationship of the couple, held on a pedestal in novels and movies, searched for by people all over the world, imagining they will reach "Nirvana," or that they'll finally be "whole" when they find their other half, that "soul mate."

I don't want to seem pessimistic or cynical because I am a big admirer of palpable love shared in a genuine relationship. Through it we learn about selfless, unconditional love, imbued with compassion, relationships which give us the courage to transform and evolve together. But it is an illusion to imagine that that particular love ideal can be instantiated by a particular person who satisfies that high expectation moment to moment. Coming to terms with the fact that ecstasy and rapture will not necessarily be found through another person, but within ourselves and through a deep connection with divinity, is related to the ability of seeing reality through the lens of the sixth chakra, beyond illusion.

CF: *Seems like this "third eye" is conspiring with divinity to our advantage. What seems particularly interesting is the possible connection our chakras make between our biological being and the universe...*

SM: True, and the seventh chakra is known as being the supreme point of connection between us and divinity. It is the crown chakra, situated on the top of our head, and is described as being a lotus with a thousand petals; it coincides not only with the integration of the other six chakras, but also with the 1000 nerves which transverse the top of our head, under the scalp. The characteristics of a well-balanced seventh chakra are the belief in a divine existence and the power of prayer, the ability to live in the moment with discernment and wisdom and to have a sharp mind, the curiosity to ask and to learn, and a strong faith in Spirit.

CF: *How would you define "Spirit"?*

SM: Perhaps as that consciousness which exists in every corner of the universe and in every cell of every organism. It is said that if the seventh chakra is not opened, God is but a myth. This energetic center is supposed to have arrived in the mass consciousness of humanity through avatars such as Jesus the Christ and Buddha, bringing a new dimension into our awareness.

Among the traumas of this chakra, forced religiosity should be mentioned, the blind acceptance of matters of spirituality and religion, where the right to question is forbidden. Deficiencies include apathy, fear that a power greater than ourselves exists, an excessive preoccupation with the first three chakras, a set of rigid convictions. An excess is manifested in the loss of identity and in religious fanaticism.

CF: *What is the ideal equilibrium of this chakra and how can it be attained?*

SM: Perhaps residing at the end of the continuum where one has a very developed ability to live in the present moment and simultaneously in continuous contact with the divine. I know of people who meditate daily, others who go on annual pilgrimages to holy places, trying in this way to get closer to God, or people who, when they become aware of their restless thoughts, try to pose their inquiries directly to God.

Of course, each one of us resides somewhere along this axis… I noticed in the case of my grandparents, all four of whom died of natural causes way into their golden years, that, as they advanced in age, they were spending more and more time connecting and even "conversing" with God and some of them even with the saints who had been part of their earlier spiritual life.

As far as I've been concerned, from an early age I felt the existence (something not shared by all the members of my family) of a Universal Spirit, although this wasn't an uninterrupted or static experience. My search has been continuous and it included a spiritual crisis when I arrived in the States in 1983, when I felt that all my points of reference were torn and I was trying desperately to hold on to something beyond material, cultural or familial values. It even included a period of atheism during my college years—funnily enough I considered myself an atheist but didn't give up the four nightly prayers I had learned from my grandmother, a source of true strength and faith throughout my life.

The search was incredibly important because I left myself exposed to many points of view, many approaches, and engaged in the informal but consistent study of several religions, in particular Buddhism, Hinduism, Judaism but also Mormonism, as I lived in Salt Lake City for eight years. I was trying to understand the common denominators of these religions, that universal essence which is not in contradiction, no matter what the religion or faith of a community.

Interestingly, a few months ago I was invited to an event titled "Good without God," organized by some dear friends, founders of a respected and thriving non-profit organization in Los Angeles. I was unable to attend and never found out if they were advocating that atheists can do just as much good or if good is not always the work of religious people, but I couldn't help thinking that all those who started such work of the heart have had an inner pull that came from up there. Are we again getting lost in semantics?

CF: *How do we find our place on earth as spiritual beings having a human experience?*

SM: The answer lies not only in the seventh chakra, but in the eighth one as well, a chakra rarely discussed and not always recognized. It is the so-called *chakra of sacred contracts.* It is said that these spiritual contracts are decided upon before we are born and they are between us and divinity, with the intention of healing ourselves and expanding our spiritual conscience. It is also said that in order for these contracts to be finalized, all needed materials and energy are put at a person's disposal.

Even though we come into the world with what is necessary in order to fulfill our contracts, we still have to develop capacities and skills that overcome apparent limitations. Of course such a contract includes elements that have to do with the ability to choose… because we always have choice, and we do not have to follow the contract.

CF: *What does such a contract look like?*

SM: For example, a sacred contract may be one agreed upon by a soul of Mahatma Gandhi's greatness, a contract through which he assumed the responsibility of completing, without violence, an action of unequaled magnitude: that of abolishing imperialism in India. Or it may be a more common type of contract, one between two souls: "In this lifetime I will be your mother, you will be my son; the lessons we will attempt to master are forgiveness and compassion." Or a contract in which the soul agrees with the Divine to make scientific discoveries that may lead to advancements in medicine, technology, etc. We often see fragments of our sacred contracts while remembering our aspirations, examining our intuitions and talents, serendipitous moments, or inner callings.

CF: *What do you think is your contract?*

SM: My belief is that all those who played an important role in my life were part of this contract, including my family and the place where I was born. Starting with my physical attributes, my talents and abilities, the paths I took and those I avoided, I know for sure they led me to the very point I find myself now: a place I know is not accidental, a place that is continuously changing but which I also try to co-create.

My sacred contract has a number of elements: to become a mother, to build an organization (Blue Heron) which contains the archetype of the parent who tries to take under its wing those whose biological parents were unable to care for them. This contract is reaffirmed day and night through the feedback I receive from the kids we help and from those supporting Blue Heron. Most likely the message of this book is part of my contract. The fact that the Universe cooperates, the fact that the strength and the resources to go on continue to show up, are all symbols which confirm that I can go on and that it is part of my calling to do it.

In the process of following this calling I have learned how to work with forces much larger than my own will. And, even though at any point in time I have the ability and freedom to choose, I've come to realize that every time I refuse an opportunity or a challenge related to my sacred contract, the consequences become harsher.

2012:
The End or a New Beginning?

CF: *There was an entire mythology concerning the end of 2012, based on the interpretation of the Mayan calendar, be it on speculations that invoke the effects of the alignment of the planets, the sun and the moon on the day of the 21st of December, be it on anecdotes launched by various groups, with or without a spiritual or religious inclination, maintaining that the time awarded to earth dwellers could reach "zero" that night… Nothing drastic happened, but do you think anything has changed?*

SM: Like others, I've read a bit on the subject of the significance of this date. Based on all the read and studied material, and based on personal intuitions and observations, I see how the phenomena of the present as well as historical time (whose stages often seem to be nonlinear jumps) represent a beginning rather than a catastrophic end of an era.

This beginning may define a certain mode of thinking and being as well as a new mode of functioning and overlapping with all that surrounds us in the physical, mental, emotional and spiritual realms. But I don't believe these changes started abruptly on December 21st 2012 ... They were set in motion years before and have accelerated recently. Of course life has continued to unfold after this date as well. It's as if we were to consider another period in history, for example the arrival of the Renaissance after the interminable Middle Ages. It didn't arrive one fine day but evolved into what it became over a number of decades.

In the Mayan culture, this transformative period is called Era Baktun, or, according to the Arizona based Hopi Indians, the passage from the fourth to the fifth world. Those who have a more spiritual nature, a more developed sixth sense, I believe, would confirm the fact that they already "feel" that the energy of the planet has been shifting, that it has become more imbued with a spiritual essence, one that is in continuous motion and evolution.

CF: *One of the key words used over and over with regards to the passage into this new era is the term transformation. What kind of transformation?*

SM: First of all, personal transformation is inseparable from global transformation. It is a transformation that helps us move beyond the limited system in which we live, where the value of our intuition, our visions, our transcendental experiences are integrated with scientific and technological methods as well as evolved social justice values, in a new paradigm.

My theory (and yes, I am an optimistic person) has a lot to do with encountering new solutions for old and complex challenges, solutions that spring out of unexpected sources, in record time, as a result of details apparently unrelated. I make this affirmation based on observations that already have taken place: from the end of the Cold War where the trust that had built between Reagan and Gorbachev played a primordial role in its finality, to the Arab Spring where the role of the social mass-media (Facebook, Youtube, Twitter, etc.) has been indisputable, to the decrease of racism due to interracial marriages. All these phenomena, apparently minor, led to the transformation of entire political and social systems which were no longer serving humanity. In the same manner, I want to hope that our generation, and the ones to come, will choose to lean toward discoveries originating from a high consciousness, toward cathartic, positive solutions.

CF: *Should we expect a positive transformation?*

SM: I think so. I attended the Maui Film Festival in 2012, where themes of spirituality were a leitmotif. One of the documentaries I watched was *2012: The Beginning*. The maker of this film traveled to six countries where she interviewed not only Mayan spiritual leaders but also archeologists, experts on hieroglyphs and authorities on cosmology. In so many words, the conclusions of the protagonists were the same: to stay open to change and get ready for a positive transformation.

CF: *Do we each have a role in provoking the change we are talking about, or do we have to subject ourselves to a transformation that will descend on us from the outside?*

SM: I would like to accentuate an idea which I believe strongly will gain a more pronounced contour in the near future—the fact that we *are all interconnected.* During the past 10-15 years, due to the Internet, we've all become especially aware of how small the world really is now; we can see with increased acceleration, and at times instantly, the results of our words and actions, and often not only in our immediate community. The reaction we may have when we wear new clothes which we find out were sewn by children working in inhumane conditions, made us take action to change laws, or "vote" by not buying those products anymore.

I am noticing that other areas of our lives are also affected. Given the fact that we are voting at least three times a day with our fork, we can start a new flux of changes as far as the food industry is concerned: how much of our food is local, organic, how much comes out of a box, how much meat (especially beef) we eat; is the food genetically modified and with little nutritional value, and how does all this relate to our physical and psychological wellbeing, as well as the wellbeing and sustainability of the farmers, the connection that many of us still want to have with the land?

The moment we extend our individual consciousness we affect changes of a universal nature. If indeed we are all one, united by a divine matrix, then what happens to me happens to everyone, and what happens for me, happens for the entire universe. Our feeling of separation is due to the illusion of duality which holds us back from seeing a ready formed unity.

CF: *I've heard talk about how the energy of the earth, the universe, would favor such profound changes on a human and planetary level... Is there danger in this?*

SM: On the contrary, I believe there is an opportunity. Indeed, the spiritual energies present on Terra are more active and thus that which is available energetically/spiritually in this period has a much stronger vibration. There are spiritual awakenings that are fast and sudden, an increasing segment of humanity has access to this transformation of consciousness, which ends up leading to the ability of our species to evolve. The fact that violence has decreased to the lowest levels in recorded history (in spite of the appearances created by the press that sensational events are the order of the day) is proof of such a change.

In the same vein of opportunities and expansion of possibilities, I am aware of the multitude of national and international catalysts that lead to solutions that uplift all of us. I could, for example, mention the TED Talks, whose motto is "Ideas Worth Spreading;" they offer information and inspiration from prestigious thinkers, scientists and doers from many fields, including technology, entertainment, social activism, design, etc.

TED has brought together a community of innovators who stimulate each other and the larger public through ideas and solutions that can influence all of humanity; its supporters passionately believe in the power of ideas to change attitudes, lives and, ultimately, the world. Even though "spirituality" is seldom if ever mentioned in their discourses, everything they do, the intentions behind the discoveries, has a profoundly human essence, and because of that, I believe, often also a profoundly spiritual essence as well.

CF: *Does humanity become more human through these transformations?*

SM: One term that keeps popping up as relating to the importance of the year 2012 is the transformation of the human species from Homo sapiens to Homo luminous, a change that it is said will take place *during* a generation and not in between. It is a term which refers to the notion of transcending into the next phase of evolution from the ability to function based predominantly on rational thinking to the capacity to rely on the heart's wisdom. It is also a term which refers to the people who function in the world using all six senses, perhaps not too far at all from the symbology of the White Magician.

CF: *I invite you then to pull out the Magician's sword!*

SM: At the level of my modest platform of influence, of small proportions, yet radiating a lot of light (or so I feel), I can clearly see that lending a helping hand—not just materially, but morally and spiritually as well—to young men and women who have been deprived of their parents' love, helps them start the transformation process from the inside out, transforming us at the same time, opening their hearts as well as ours, giving themselves—and, by witnessing them, us—the hope of a second chance and a renewed faith in life. We've helped give them the opportunity for a dignified place in society, and in turn we have the opportunity to occupy a more dignified place within ourselves.

The fact that almost every year, of the 90 young men and women we assist, 9 are in medical school (one student was even tied to the crib the first three years of his life in a deplorable orphanage) seems to me nothing short of a miracle, which in the future will be multiplied many fold, not only by us, but by them as well, the kids we've touched.

We've all had the experience that it is possible, that we are capable of being the initiators of these miracles, and from now on we're expecting that they happen with some regularity, as if it was something "normal." On my personal and perhaps limited scale, I'm not wasting my time wondering "What will we feed the eight billion Earth inhabitants?" but instead I wonder "what miracles can I create tomorrow?"

Unexpected non-linear progress and creative solutions are sprouting up in many vital areas, it is hard to believe that with the focused intention and determinations of so many high-minded individuals, the balance of humanity will not shift toward the good.

In this way, as we allow ourselves to be guided by our Higher Self, or the White Magician as I like to call it, I am convinced that, directly or indirectly, the great challenges for humanity will be dealt with at the right time and in the right way by people whose abilities and sacred contracts will play crucial and irreplaceable roles in the collage which influences humanity's destiny on Earth.

Epilogue

"You see, I hate to say it, but it's true that I am not a really good academic. For me, intellectual work is related to what you could call "aestheticism," meaning transforming yourself.... I know very well, and I think I knew it from the moment when I was a child, that knowledge can do nothing for transforming the world. Maybe I am wrong. And I am sure I am wrong from a theoretical point of view... You see, that's why I really work like a dog, and I worked like a dog all my life. I am not interested in the academic status of what I am doing because my problem is my own transformation... This transformation of one's self by one's own knowledge is, I think, something rather close to the aesthetic experience. Why should a painter work if he is not transformed by his own painting?"
— Michel Foucault

After the launch of *Searching for the White Magician* in its Romanian version in several U.S. and Romanian cities and the success of its second edition, I was encouraged to translate it into English. Time passed. I was dragging my feet. My main concern was whether this book would have a place in the U.S., if this voice and this filter of the world had any value in the American context. There was something else at work too, a murmur which slowly became a crescendo. Since the publication of the Romanian version in 2012, I had arrived at another crossroads, a place in space and time that felt like a centrifuge which spun me and spat me out armed with a suit of practicality, realism and a strengthened instinct for the bottom line. Could the cause have been the intensity of the college admissions process that we experienced with our sons? Or the aftermath of astronomic convergences—those big but gradual changes predicted to unfold after the much anticipated year 2012? Or the advances in IT, artificial intelligence, the pervasiveness of smartphones? Or the more efficient, more accessible but less personal services ranging from online banking and online shopping to online sex?

I cannot pinpoint just one source, but what I can say for sure is that this new direction is loaded with a great deal of realism and pragmatism which I feel I cannot ignore. I've become aware of a bigger level of competition in the world around me, from how hard it has become to raise money for the foundation I run, to the incredible pressures experienced by our sons to succeed at their respective schools and to "make something of themselves." In addition, I've experienced a compelling demonstration in our surroundings of a new paradigm: that in which the results are more important than the process. Sometimes, in fact, the process doesn't seem to matter at all. There was a sense inside me that ignoring these new trends could potentially sabotage my trajectory toward certain concrete goals.

Concomitantly and seemingly out of the blue, I became more interested in the stock market and have since followed and invested diligently in a handful of carefully picked stocks, mainly tech and pharma, making a respectable return on my investment. I've quite enjoyed following those numbers, researching the companies and their CEOs, attending the annual TED Talks in Canada and engaging with the market in a way that felt self-empowering.

One other program I engaged in was a six-month coaching project to improve my nutritional habits and fitness level. To that extent, I committed to a minimum of five intense workouts a week while minimizing certain foods in my diet—such as single carbs and meats—in an effort to step into a more vibrant physical self. To commit to the spiritual path doesn't mean that we disconnect from or ignore the physical level, be it our monetary situation or our physical health. One of the wise sayings I concur with is that our body is the temple of our soul, and we should treat it as such. To that end, I committed to this six-month process with excitement and dedication and was thrilled when, at its completion, I had achieved my goals. To this day I continue to maintain the habits.

As far as the non-profit I run, the pragmatism is reflected in the process of keeping our finger on the pulse of what is going on in the world of nonprofits and continuously adapting and fine-tuning our fund-raising strategies in order to retain our competitive edge. We are also constantly attuned to what is going on in Romania and the Republic of Moldova, so that we can position ourselves strategically and help in the most meaningful and profound ways. For example, in Romania we always keep searching for the most deserving kids who live in the most underserved and poorest areas; in order to achieve that objective, we penetrate into new regions where our program is needed the most. The same goes for Moldova, not only the poorest country in Europe but also the country with the highest rate of human trafficking in the region, the place where only a 9th grade education is mandatory and where so many promising, competent teenagers are stuck or lost at the tender age of 15. So, we are pragmatic about what needs to change on an ongoing basis. And we are practical and realistic about what we expect from our students in an effort to help them become responsible, independent adults. So yes, our spirit is strong, and our mission does come from that higher place—we find youth with broken wings, take them under our wing and ultimately help them fly—but we are very serious about the actual steps they need to take almost daily in order for them to take flight and soar.

All of the above being said, the skills I've learned while earning a Master's in Applied Spiritual Psychology, the deep connection with my inner journey and the interest in the subtle laws of the unseen, continue to be a big component in my life. In fact, they are such a big part of my modus operandi, so easily and naturally incorporated in my every day way of being, that I don't have to put them on my schedule anymore or check them off of a list. I remember my dreams almost every morning—I reflect on them; I meditate daily or weekly, as needed; I stop and contemplate when I have to slow down. I close my eyes and do a quick self-forgiving process as I wait at a red light. I send light to the cashier on the spot, if I sense she needs it that day. Faith is ingrained in me too; it's almost always there, I don't have to work so hard at cultivating it. But the layer of pragmatism is now also there, this updated and energized layer of navigating the physical world reality according to the rules made by our fellow countrymen and fellow global citizens of the 21st century.

In the end, we want to make choices that are for our highest good, choices of a high vibration. Ultimately, all of us are souls who chose to take on an incarnation, to live in a physical body. Thus, we have to make conscious decisions that will protect our safety, our health, our livelihood and that of others. I am very clear that one cannot successfully navigate life when only Maslow's top tier of the pyramid is cared for[7]—an erroneous assumption sometimes made by those who seek to understand the spiritual

[7] Abraham Maslow propounded his theory of a hierarchy of needs in a 1943 paper. The theory is often portrayed in the shape of a pyramid with the most fundamental, physiological needs at the bottom and the more abstract need for self-actualization and self-transcendence at the top.

realms. We want to make sure that our decisions positively affect all other levels: that our physiological and safety needs are cared for, that we feel we belong and are loved, that our esteem, our cognitive and aesthetic needs, are honored along with self-actualization and (hopefully) transcendence.

As far as where we are in these times, perceived as turbulent by many, especially since the 2016 elections, I am observing that fighting what we disagree with or perceive as offensive by using "against-ness" is doing exactly the same thing the "other side" is doing. In other words, it is counter-productive to be "against violence." The way to be is "for peace." Standing for "inclusiveness" is more powerful than standing for "anti-segregation." "Peace" is more powerful than "anti-war." *We always move in the direction of what we emphasize*, that is the law observed in spiritual psychology. For me personally the most powerful message I can put out there at this time is to be and embody that which I want to see more of in the world. To that effect, I'm dedicated to cultivating my generosity, my altruism, my tolerance, my song and poetry, and to allowing my actions to speak louder than words.

Stefania Magidson

Stefania Magidson was born in Brasov, Romania, and in 1983 immigrated with her family to the United States. She received a B.S. in Health Education from University of Utah and worked for the Utah State Health Department, Centers for Disease Control. She later received a Master of Arts in Applied Psychology from University of Santa Monica with a post-master specialization in "Consciousness, Health and Healing."

Inspired by the Los Angeles based Everychild Foundation, in 2002 she founded Blue Heron Foundation, a non-profit charitable organization whose mission is to improve the quality of life of Romanian and Moldovan orphaned and abandoned youth and provide them greater access to life's opportunities by awarding them college scholarships. The organization has raised over $1,800,000, has awarded over 300 college scholarships and touched the lives of over 3,000 kids (www.blueheronfoundation.org). Stefania is a supporter of artistic and social causes, film festivals, theater and film productions as well as other cultural events.

She is an active Los Angeles resident, involved in supporting the UCLA Graduate School of Education, NYU's Tisch School of the Arts, The Everychild Foundation, the South East European Film Festival

(Los Angeles) and Making Waves Romanian Film Festival (New York). She served as a translator for the documentary *Monica and Gabriel* (2015) and produced the upcoming film *Omega Rose* (2018).

Stefania lives in Los Angeles with her husband and their two sons.

≈

Romanian born **Carmen Firan** is a poet, novelist, journalist, playwright and screenplay writer. She set roots in New York City after serving as program director for the Romanian Cultural Institute N.Y. (1997 to 2001). Among the most recent books she published in the United States are *Interviews and Encounters* (Poems and dialogue with Nina Cassian, Sheep Meadow Press), *Inferno* (SD Press), *Rock and Dew* (Sheep Meadow Press) and *Words and Flesh* (Talisman Publishers). Her work appears in magazines, anthologies and books in France, Israel, Sweden, Germany, England, Ireland, Poland. She is a member of the Writers Union (Romania), The Poetry Society of America and PEN American Center (New York).

70084890R00102

Made in the USA
San Bernardino, CA
24 February 2018